HOPE
IN THE
MOURNING

Hope in the Mourning

Dedicated to my grandparents, Burton and Dolores Michaelson,
who taught me that joy and sorrow are often mingled in this life,
but when our circumstances drive us to the feet of Jesus,
life can be sweet indeed.

REVIEWS

The suffering Christ is the focal point for every Christian. The crucified Christ is our vision. For Him, the path to glory was the path of suffering. And that is the pattern for us. Our suffering leads to greater sanctification and to greater glory. In *Hope in the Mourning*, Emily Curtis has compiled twenty-one stories of suffering saints who exemplify this biblical truth. In addition to firsthand accounts, you will also find practical advice on how to minister to those who are suffering. I trust you will be encouraged by these stories of God's faithfulness in the midst of suffering.

John MacArthur, Pastor, Grace Community Church

The Psalms are a fountain that God's people have continually gone to for drinks of encouragement in difficult times. Besides being inspired truth, one of the appealing features of many psalms is transparency. David is especially known for honestly conveying his struggles with faith, doubt, pain, and failure. Yet, he is also known for landing on his feet as he regularly counseled himself to 'hope in God' (Psalm 42:11). The chapters in *Hope in the Mourning* remind me of those various psalms in which the psalmist does not hold back articulating his struggles, but also in which he is willing to pass along the lessons learned. Each chapter in this compilation by Emily Curtis is an account by someone who has faced the kind of hardship and suffering that can tempt even a follower of Christ to feel crushed by sorrow. The various authors openly share their journeys with a refreshing candidness that readers will appreciate. But most important, they clearly share the timeless truths that brought them through the dark valleys.

Each account in *Hope in the Mourning* is filled with testimony to the goodness of God, even when life hurts. An additional, unique feature is the Hope & Helps section at the end of each chapter. The authors use these sections as an opportunity to offer practical advice as to what they found most helpful: the Bible passages they turned to, the songs they listened to, and even the acts of kindness expressed by friends. In addition, the authors give insight into the type of statements that others ought to avoid when trying to minister to someone going through a difficult time.

Emily has done the church a great service in assembling the various stories in *Hope in the Mourning*. And the addition of her own poems provides even more food for thought and encouragement for the soul.

I am, or have been, the pastor to many of these individuals who have chosen to share their stories in *Hope in the Mourning*. So I know firsthand of their striving to persevere in times of pain and doubt. And I personally witnessed how the Lord's comfort became a balm to their hearts. They were an encouragement to my wife and me as we observed their faith winning out over their sense of loss or discouragement or heartache. I am therefore confident that those who are in the midst of great struggles, or who feel like the waves of life's trials are overwhelming them, will find hope in the midst of their disappointment, their pain, even in their mourning by reading this helpful collection of narratives.

Carey Hardy, Pastor, Twin City Bible Church

Emily Curtis's compilation of heartfelt personal accounts of loss which lead to deeper more meaningful relationships with Christ is a window into a richer connection with God for any reader! I personally found the Hope & Helps sections at the end of each story of hope incredibly useful for any of us who mean well but need assistance navigating these delicate conversations.

Tammie Wiley, MD, Winston-Salem Pediatrics

The last thing a person who is deeply grieving needs is a room full of chatty people or a standard-length book with point A and point B and a study guide that follows.

Emily Curtis has captured exactly what someone who has suffered great loss needs in those moments when even close friends aren't enough.

This book is a collection: a cornucopia of Scripture, hymns, sweet stories of God's comforting grace. In 2014, my wife of almost 45 years stepped into heaven. That's my story of loss. Maybe it's yours, too. Or it might be the story of someone you love who has suffered indescribable loss.

Emily's book hadn't been published when Bobbie died in 2014. But if it had, this book would have been exactly what I would have needed.

Thank you, Emily. Your book is a gift.

Robert Wolgemuth
Best-selling author of *Finish Line:*
Dispelling Fear, Finding Peace,
and Preparing for the End of Your Life

As a Pastor, I am regularly faced with the privileged ministry of coming alongside people or families traveling the road of suffering. I have witnessed the power of the scriptures being a balm to the wounded and weary soul, and I am thankful for the sufficiency of the Bible. And I am also grateful for the testimony of people who have persevered through trials by God's grace and His Word. In *Hope in the Mourning*, Emily Curtis has provided an anthology of powerful stories from ordinary people suffering extraordinary hardships who found hope and healing from God's presence and Word.

The compelling stories brought me to tears, made me smile, took me into deep periods of contemplation, but most of all, caused me to thank God for His comforting and sustaining grace. The breadth and scope of the twenty-one stories broaden the book's potential reach. The format is helpful, and I suspect the practical tips at the end of each section will serve many people who desire to walk with suffering friends and/ or families but do not know exactly what to say or do. I can see this book used in the church by pastors and counselors for a long time.

Anthony Kidd, Pastor of Preaching, Community of Faith Bible Church

As a physician, I see many people go through very difficult health crises. This book reminds me that those who focus on the Lord—not to the exclusion of their circumstances but more on Him than all else—they are the ones who ultimately "renew their strength and mount up with wings like eagles.

Jeff D. Williamson, MD, MHS, Professor of Gerontology and Geriatric Medicine, Atrium Health Wake Forest Baptist

Oh how thankful I am for a volume like this which you now hold in your hand! *Hope in the Mourning* resonates with my heart because over a short span of time I personally experienced seven deaths within my own family. It has been the most trying and difficult season of my forty-year Christian life. Over the past 15 years, I've experienced approximately one death every two years, including my step-father, my mother, my newborn grandson, my wife, my only sister, my favorite aunt and my mother-in-law.

Each of these deaths became a series of severe trials for which I, myself, was rocked and pummeled. As both a pastor and a counselor, I now had to become the determined recipient of all that I had previously taught and shared with so many others, drawing for myself such vital, biblical principles for a heart wracked with unimaginable grief and sorrow. I can now honestly say to you, dear fellow sufferer, that it is these very sweet principles of God's Word, plus the loving care of God's people, which have been the balm to sustain me during such tumultuous seasons.

As you read through this beautiful book, which seeks to encourage you in your own seasons of hurt, pain, and loss (or perhaps what has occurred to others you both love and cherish and now want to help), may these precious pages become a tangible reminder to you of how God rejoices to take up His spiritual children into His loving arms, especially when the hurting comes.

Lance Quinn, Pastoral Team, Grace Immanuel Bible Church & Vice-President, The Expositors Seminary

ACKNOWLEDGMENTS

This book would not have been possible without the honest testimonies of dear Christian brothers and sisters. They willingly poured out their hearts for the benefit of others and I'm forever grateful for the privilege of sharing their stories.

My editor, Scott Lang, edited each precious story with thought and care. I'm so thankful that the Lord provided someone who happened to know many of the writers to edit their most intimate stories. He patiently walked me through many book-related questions and helped make the book richer and more beautiful.

The book designer, Jon Kaya, brought life and character to the design. He paid attention to every detail and worked for many months to create a book that will be a lasting treasure to its readers. He brought to fruition a design that points to the goodness of God and to His peace that is greater than our circumstances.

I'm thankful for my husband, Brent, and my children, Micah, Avia, Malachi and Alayah for encouraging me in this project and allowing me time to focus on it over the past couple of years.

Most importantly, I'm thankful for a gracious Savior who brought these wonderful people into my life, laid this book on my heart, and paved the path to bring it to completion. My prayer is that He is glorified through this book and that many find a hope and a refuge in Him by reading *Hope in the Mourning*.

All profits from *Hope in the Mourning* go toward bereavement ministries.

Hope in the Mourning
A Hope-Filled Guide Through Grief

Copyright © 2023 Emily Curtis

Design and production: Jon Kaya
Editor: Scott Lang

ISBN-13: 978-1-954437-88-3

✝CSP

Carpenter's Son Publishing
307 Verde Meadow Drive
Franklin, TN 37067
United States of America

Scripture taken from the NEW AMERICAN STANDARD BIBLE®,
Copyright © 1960,1962,1963,1968,1971,1972,1973,1975,1977,1995
by The Lockman Foundation. Used by permission.
Scripture quotations marked (ESV) are from the ESV® Bible
(The Holy Bible, English Standard Version®), copyright © 2001 by Crossway,
a publishing ministry of Good News Publishers.
Used by permission. All rights reserved.

23   24   25   26   27   28   HM   6   5   4   3   2   1

CONTENTS

PREFACE

Friends,

What a journey this book has been. In 2016, a college friend of mine (and writer in this book) posted on Facebook that her husband of 6 weeks was in a terrible accident and had passed away from his injuries. Shocked and heartbroken for my friend, I remember wanting desperately to comfort her in some way. How do you comfort someone thousands of miles away? How do you reconnect with someone that you have only interacted with on social media for the last decade? I wanted to reach out to her, but also feared that I might say the wrong thing. I called the wisest person I know, my grandmother, and asked for advice. She encouraged me to reach out and simply show my friend love in any way possible. That Christmas, I sent her a gift box with a blanket and necklace filled with charms representing special moments in her husband's life along with notes and Scriptures gathered from fellow Christians. This was the birth of Gifts of Hope. A small company with a heart to minister to the hurting and help you feel confident in connecting with your grieving loved ones.

Little did I know what amazing people God would place before me through this ministry. Story after story crossed my path of unthinkable losses mingled with incomprehensible hope and joy. Treasures of insight were given to me by these special people who let me into their grief and taught me how to show compassion in an active and deep way. It was pressed onto my heart again and again that even Jesus wept when his friend Lazarus died. He wept not only for his loss, but he wept with Mary and Martha as they mourned the death of their brother. Jesus knew He was going to raise Lazarus from the dead, yet he wept.

This struck me. How often do we shy away from those who are deep in grief? It's uncomfortable and I think we all share the same fear of saying or doing the wrong thing. I learned through my new friends that saying nothing is far more painful. As humans we tend to shy away from those who are grieving and as Christians we often unintentionally minimize suffering by throwing out verses thoughtlessly and offering trite platitudes. We "celebratize" those who mourn by ushering them onto speaking platforms before we have tended thoroughly to the healing of their hearts.

One of the most poignant things a friend (and writer in this book) said to me is, "Sometimes we simply need to sit in the ashes with those who mourn and mourn alongside them. Then, when they are ready, offer them a hand up and gently walk beside them."

These stories will allow you to lean into the suffering of the authors, and will help equip you to purposefully mourn with, and meaningfully minister to, those suffering in your midst. Each chapter tells of personal heartache and God's amazing grace. The stories are followed by responses to what was most—and least—helpful during difficult days. That feature is intended to help you know how to best serve others in similar situations.

None of these stories were written by seasoned authors. Rather, they are an honest outpouring of grieving hearts who have experienced God's deepest graces and mercies in the darkest of situations. These writers, like you, have walked through tumultuous terrain. Their faith has been challenged and they have found a beautiful gem of hope in their suffering—hope in the One who is ever present, whose mercies are new each morning (Lamentations 3:22–23).

They are people like you and me with grief as unique as their stories, yet they've all shared in the goodness of God, who is never changing; He is the same God in each circumstance. He is the God who sees, the God who formed their inward parts, the God who grants peace beyond understanding and the God who loves His children fiercely.

May this book serve as a useful tool in growing each of us as we carry out in obedience the command to "rejoice with those who rejoice and mourn with those who mourn" (Romans 12:15). May you see our God with fresh and thankful eyes and may you seek to be His hands and feet to every weary heart.

Through each story, my prayer is that your heart finds renewed courage and that you see hope in the mourning.

Praying for you,
Emily Curtis

FOREWORD BY
JONI EARECKSON TADA

———

Before you begin … just breathe.

I stared at those words, emotion choking my chest. Someone had stopped their car on the side of a country road, gotten out and picked up pieces of roadside gravel. Bending over the black asphalt, they arranged small white stones into those two short words: Just breathe. My eyes rested on the gentle command, and then I looked far into the distance where the road disappeared. I blinked back tears. Sometimes the grief and pain seem to go on forever, just like that country road. And all you can do is, just breathe.

Losses touch us in many shapes and sizes, and each loss brings with it a unique grief. Perhaps you've lost a precious loved one, a life partner, or a child. You've lost the hope of marriage. Your grief could be a devastating blow to your reputation. Or an unexpected divorce. Maybe older age has robbed you of good health. Perhaps you are trying to cope with a life-altering injury, such as I experienced when I broke my neck. Whatever you must let go of, the wounds could be raw and tender; or they could be chronic and scarred over. It doesn't matter. The pain is heartbreakingly yours.

I experience it daily. After so much time, it's still hard to wake up in the morning and just breathe. Fifty years ago, when I became a quadriplegic in a diving accident, I could not bear to hear well-meaning comments such as, "Joni, your paralysis will make you a stronger person," or "Don't worry, time will heal all things." It may have been true, but at the moment, what I needed was strength to wake up and move into the day.

Thank the Lord, God gave that strength through friends who mostly sat with me and prayed. Listening to my laments, they ran their gentle fingers over the fissures in my heart, took a risk and … reached out. Some tenderly pushed Scripture into my anguish. Others read stories about saints who suffered. Most simply spent time with me: on the back porch at night looking at stars or by our farmhouse fireplace listening to music.

Some friends devised wonderfully creative ways of offering encouragement. One young woman baked my favorite zucchini bread every month, then brought it warm in a basket with a thermos of hot tea—as we ate together, she read from a small book of poetry. Another wrote weekly notes, tucking in handwritten prayers. Still another took me on "wheelchair hikes" every month—somehow we'd always end up on a hill overlooking a vista where we would pause and pray. All these things and more gave me strength to face the day. Then month.

Then year. After that, I could wake up without being overwhelmed by sad feelings. I had learned how to breathe. And even smile.

Tim Keller wisely observed that "the joy of the Lord doesn't come after the sorrow. It does not come after the weeping. The weeping drives you into the joy, and it enhances the joy, and then the joy enables you to actually feel your grief without it sinking you. And then you find you are finally emotionally healthy."

After more than 50 years of living in a wheelchair, I recall with great affection those dear friends who lifted me out of depression through their unique encouragements. And like them, I try to do the same when I encounter people who have suffered loss. I try to reach out. Show them Jesus, offer hand-tailored encouragement, and help them to just breathe.

One of the ways I do this is with Emily Curtis's *Gifts of Hope*—in fact, right before penning these words, I sent one to a loved one who just suffered a stroke and broken hip. It included artesian bottles of fragrant teas, a beautiful poem, a few items of comfort and my personal message hand-crafted on parchment paper. The gift is unique. It's charming. And it reminds me of that warm zucchini bread and chamomile tea given at a different time and place. I do believe Emily's offering will bolster my stroke-surviving friend—it should; the *Gifts of Hope* team are praying for her.

Emily understands how to help those with wounded hearts. She is the compassionate and talented granddaughter of my longtime friends, Burton and Dolores Michaelson. Through *Gifts of Hope*, Emily has met many people who are grieving and suffering— she is helping their friends reach out and offer hand-fashioned encouragement which delights the soul and the senses. Over time, Emily has collected a treasure trove of astounding stories that showcase overcoming grace, sacrificial love, and undaunted courage. Not to waste any divine opportunity, she has gathered these testimonies in this remarkable new book you hold in your hands, *Hope in the Mourning*.

As you read the heartwarming stories of people on these pages, you will understand that in time, the waves of grief actually do quell and calm a bit. Those waves still—I think they always will—swell up occasionally into a storm of emotion, but even then, our blessed Savior can calm that sea. And should I be describing you; if grief ebbs and flows in your heart, I pray the stories on the following pages will be refreshing, helping you see that there is hope in your mourning.

So, welcome to the chapters of this exceptional book. Welcome to what it means to breathe in the Breath of Life who heals our deepest hurts.

Joni Eareckson Tada
Joni and Friends International Disability Center

Mingled Joy

John Martin

It is doubtful whether God can bless a man greatly until he has hurt him deeply.
—A.W. Tozer

In October of 2013, after seven years of struggle trying to conceive a baby—that included five miscarriages—the Lord gave my wife, Lisa, and me a daughter. We were ecstatic and thankful. Two years later, the Lord gave us another daughter. Grace upon grace. After a season of loss our arms were full. We had our two beautiful girls and our little family was complete. Then, in the summer of 2018 my wife pulled me aside one afternoon and said, "I need to talk to you." It's a good thing I was sitting down because I wasn't prepared for what she would say next. I had been dealing with challenges at my job for a couple of years and was unsure about our financial future. We had been married 15 years and weren't as young as we used to be. We had toddlers running around the house at a time when our friends were getting ready to send their kids to college. We were tired. For all the years we had asked the Lord for children, hearing my wife say "I'm pregnant" that afternoon sent me into a tailspin thinking of all the reasons we weren't prepared for a third baby. My insecurities were exposed and I was suddenly an unwilling, white-knuckled passenger on a rollercoaster I had no control over. God was beginning to reveal my pride and self-sufficiency.

A few months later we found out that we were having a boy and his due date was on March 15, 2019, my fortieth birthday. I was excited to have a son and I had started to settle into the idea of becoming a family of five. I still had concerns for Lisa's health and the baby's development. Lisa's second pregnancy had come with complications, and at one point the doctor had told us that our daughter would be born with serious birth defects. But this pregnancy looked exactly as it was supposed to and Lisa's doctor was using terms like "textbook" to describe how well things were going. The day before Thanksgiving, Lisa had an appointment with her doctor and was given the all-clear to travel to my mom and dad's house for the holiday weekend. At 24 weeks pregnant, both mom and baby were looking healthy and on track.

The next day we made the 100-mile drive to the rural area where my parents have lived for nearly 50 years. We had a restful day with family and reflected on how grateful we were for the good report we'd received from Lisa's doctor the day prior. After family and friends left, we settled in by the fire and watched a movie with our girls. At about 10 pm Lisa said she was feeling fatigued and that the baby had worked his way into an uncomfortable position. Neither of us were too concerned. The baby tended to be very active at evening time and it wasn't unusual for Lisa to feel some discomfort as a result. She was feeling some tension but chalked it up to mild Braxton Hicks (false labor) contractions which she had experienced when pregnant with each of our girls. We went to bed expecting things to resolve with rest.

At around 2 am, Lisa woke me up and said, "Something's wrong … we need to call the doctor." Mild discomfort had quickly escalated into something much more intense and regular. The doctor told us to get Lisa to the closest hospital with a maternity ward. I woke up my parents to let them know we would need to leave the girls, and moments later we were on our way to the nearest hospital, 25 minutes away. The same hospital, in fact, where I had been born nearly 40 years prior.

By the time we arrived at the hospital it was clear that Lisa was in full-blown labor. Her contractions were two minutes apart and so intense she couldn't talk through them. She struggled to walk into the ER, where a nurse immediately recognized what was happening and rushed us into triage. Upon examination, another nurse told us that Lisa was dilated to six centimeters and that the hospital wasn't equipped to handle a premature infant. We would need to find a hospital willing to take the baby upon delivery. Lisa was hurried into a delivery room. A local doctor was paged and on the way. Meanwhile the nurses were doing everything possible to slow down labor and increase the baby's chance of survival. The contractions became acute and frequent. Lisa was in extreme pain.

A little later we were told that a nearby hospital would admit our son and had deployed a highly specialized NICU response team. They were about an hour out. But our little man wasn't waiting and things began to move very quickly. When the doctor arrived, he promptly informed us that our baby probably wouldn't survive and that a C-section delivery would be risky for my wife. I asked him if we had any other options. "No," he said.

And just like that, they escorted me into an empty OR waiting room and wheeled my wife through the large double doors down the hall. What followed was the longest 20 minutes of my life. I was completely cutoff. I prayed for my wife and my baby boy, not knowing what might be ahead for either of them. I would learn later that just before sedation for surgery, Lisa's water broke. Over the hospital speakers an urgent call echoed through the halls, "Code blue, code blue! OR 1!" Virtually every staff member rushed in to assist. Minutes later our little boy was born at around 4:30 am on Friday morning, November 23, weighing 1 pound, 9 ounces. Sixteen weeks early. Severely premature.

Our son had to be resuscitated twice upon delivery. In the moments that followed I watched at least ten nurses and doctors provide life-sustaining care. Eventually we were told that his heart rate was ok but his eyes were fused shut. Moments later we were told that he had opened one eye, and then that he had opened both eyes and looked around. Our little man was fighting. A couple of hours later he was stable enough to transport. The team of caregivers wheeled him to Lisa's bedside so we could spend a minute together before they took him away.

Sitting there with Lisa and our tiny baby boy was the sweetest and most painful moment that morning. Joy mingled with heartbreak and fear of the unknown. And that would become a theme as our son's life hung in the balance day by day, for the next several months. We would end up moving our family 100 miles from home to be close to the NICU. I lost my job as a result. Every anxious insecurity I had months earlier now seemed small in the face of such an insurmountable reality. God had thrust us into the awareness of our frailty and dependence, and it was humbling. It was excruciating and hard. But it was also sweet, as we learned more about the manifest love of Christ through the church than we ever had before.

We named our son Jack Henry, in honor of his great-grandfathers. Jack earned a reputation in his unit as "the littlest baby with the biggest opinions." He was a fighter. The Lord sustained him through 182 days in the NICU. Six months, three hospitals, three major surgeries, multiple transfusions, intubation and PICC (peripherally inserted central catheter) lines, an endless line of doctors, nurses, specialists, and therapists—and countless evidence of God's kindness in the process. Having lost my job and benefits, I was preparing for the potential of losing our home and declaring bankruptcy. But God provided. And even after what would be around 6 million dollars in medical expenses, every need was met.

We were regularly warned of the dire outcomes associated with being a 24-week micro preemie: blindness, deafness, lung and heart disease, cerebral palsy, to name a few. While Jack is not without challenges due to his prematurity, he exceeded expectations in every way. Today, he is growing and getting stronger, regularly impressing his team of specialists. To hold Jack in my arms is to be gifted with a living reminder of the Father's kindness. It was His kindness that took us into the deepest valley of our lives so that we could be broken and watch Him provide. And His kindness remained with us in the cold, dark, lonely moments of grief when all we could understand was the hurt.

God wants us to grieve when hard things happen. He wants us to express our sorrow to Him. Solomon says in Ecclesiastes 3 that there is a time for everything: "For everything there is a season and a time for every matter under heaven: a time to be born, and a time to die … a time to break down, and a time to build up; a time to weep, and a time to laugh; a time to mourn, and a time to dance."

Through the trauma and uncertainty, the Lord graciously taught us to lament. To take our sorrow, fear, questions, pain, hope, and faith to Him; crying out in prayer and pouring our hearts out to the Rock of Ages, who is the anchor and refuge for our souls. We learned to keep nothing from the One who sees all, acknowledging our struggle while striving for faith-filled reflection on His character and purposes. We took comfort in the Psalms, a treasure trove of Godward lament of which one commentator notes, "The very presence of such prayers in Scripture is a witness to God's understanding. He knows how men speak when they are desperate."

God does not take us around the pain. He takes us through it. But we can be sure that our grief is never final. In Christ, death gives way to life. Beauty from ashes, joy from mourning, and praise from despair. We're thankful for how God has chosen to bless Jack, but every day we strive to find our rest in His merciful character and sovereign will rather than our circumstances. Whatever the future holds, God is good and His ways are perfect. He is trustworthy and we are blessed. Our hearts are filled with thankfulness.

Baby Jack
December 2018

Jack goes home — May 2019

Jack with sisters.
Ella & Rose — 2020

God does not take us around the pain.
He takes us through it.
But we can be sure that our grief is never final.
In Christ, death gives way to life.
Beauty from ashes, joy from mourning,
and praise from despair.

HOPE & HELPS

Scripture we clung to on the hardest days/nights:
Matthew 12:20; Matthew 6:26–34; Romans 8:28, 35; Romans 11:33–36; Psalm 30:5; Psalm 34:18; 1 Peter 5:10; Isaiah 55:8–9; Isaiah 41:10; Job 12:10; Lamentations 3:22–23

Helpful ways people ministered to us:
- Anticipated and met various needs without being asked.
- Helped us find a longer-term place to stay near the hospital, negotiated terms, and made sure it was furnished and comfortable.
- Wept with us, rejoiced with us, and paid attention to the details.
- Regularly sent comforting scriptures and specific prayers, without expectation of response.
- Provided fellowship and support that recognized a greater context than our trial.
- Organized meals without us needing to be involved and then checked-in as time went on to assure the need was being met effectively.
- Thought of our girls and sent goodies, gifts, games, and activities to keep them occupied and cared for.
- Came to the hospital just to be present and pray.
- Brought snacks, water, and coffee to the hospital.
- Committed to regular babysitting so our girls had consistency.
- Provided gift cards for restaurants, grocery stores, coffee shops and gas stations.

What you should NOT say to someone in a similar circumstance:
- It's natural to want to relate to someone with a similar experience or story but, generally speaking, this is unhelpful. One person's story is not a prescriptive of someone else's and comparison can lead to false hope or unrealistic expectations. Every situation is unique, and so are God's purposes.
- You don't know what the outcome will be, so please don't act as though you do. You may feel confident that God is going to do a miracle, but it's better to communicate that you are praying to that end instead of saying that you "know" it will happen.
- "Let me know how I can help. Please call/text if I can do anything for you." This approach, though usually well intentioned, misses the mark in several big ways. First, it puts the burden on the sufferer to figure out what they need, when they need it, and who can provide for it. Second, it puts the sufferer in the position of having to ask for more when they already feel weak, needy, overwhelmed, and sometimes overexposed. This makes the sufferer feel like a burden to others. Lastly, it doesn't seem sincere and can be the opposite of your intended effect. It's helpful to mention what you'd like to do and ask about the day, time, and place instead of

asking if you can do the thing and when. It's the difference between, "Can I come clean your house on Thursday?" and "I'd like to come clean your house, can I come Thursday?" The second makes the sufferer feel like less of a burden.

- Don't be offended if your offer to help is not responded to immediately or at all. It's likely that many others are offering as well and needs are being met.

- Scripture is the best source of comfort, hope, encouragement, correction, and truth. But Scripture is not a band-aid that removes pain and fixes struggles. Pat theological talking points or verses out of context feel like you're trying to fix or dismiss the problem instead of enduring and walking alongside.

We don't expect you to understand, have answers, or relate to our situation. Expressions of love, prayers, and care are far more comforting. It's also helpful when you mention specifically what you are praying for or simply pass along a comforting scripture. Weep and lament with the sufferer, then sing with them to the God of all comfort and grace.

- Some sufferers find it helpful and comforting to talk about details and specifics. Some find it invasive. Always be willing to talk, ask, and listen. But don't be pushy.

- When you're in crisis mode it can be difficult to find time, energy, and brain space to read scripture extensively. Often it's the scripture and songs that are hidden in your heart that sustain, reassures and take up residence in your mind. Don't ask or expect that the sufferer is able to study but rather ask how the Lord is encouraging and sustaining them.

- Read the room. That's a helpful phrase for all of life but especially when you're with someone in a trial. Be aware of how they're feeling and act appropriately. Having fun and laughing can be good medicine but if it's at an inappropriate time it can be salt in the wound. Levity and sober-mindedness both have a place in encouraging the sufferer.

Hymns or songs that comforted us:
- *Great Is Thy Faithfulness*, Thomas Chisholm and William Runyan
- *Love That Will Not Let Me Go*, George Matheson
- *I Need Thee Every Hour*, Annie Sherwood Hawks (1836–1918), Robert Lowry (1826–1899)
- *Day by Day*, Lina Sandell, Translated by A. L. Skoog, Oscar Ahnfeldt
- *Dear Refuge of My Weary Soul*, Anne Steele (1716–1778)
- *He Will Hold Me Fast*, Original words vv. 1-2 by Ada Habershon, new words and music by Matt Merker
- *Christ the Sure and Steady Anchor*, Matt Boswell and Matt Papa
- *Lord from Sorrows Deep I Call*, Matt Boswell and Matt Papa
- *Hide Away in the Love of Jesus*, Steve and Vikki Cook

- *In the Valley*, Music and words by Bob Kauflin. Based on prayer from *The Valley of Vision* by Arthur Bennett

The hope Jesus has given us through our trial:
Our God hears us and answers prayers. His answers are always best. He doesn't always give us what we ask for, but He always gives us Himself. He doesn't promise ease or health or easy outcomes, but He does promise to draw near, comfort, protect, provide, and conquer death and the grave.

He began teaching us about hope during our years of waiting and loss. It became so clear to us that our hope could not be in having children, or in seeing the end of the trial, or even in having answers to our whys. Our true hope and delight can only be found in Him. Every other hope falls short and disappoints.

Hope in Him is confidence. Hope in Him is joy. Hope in Him is sure and steady. That kind of hope holds you secure on the mountain top and deep valley alike. We hope for the future glory that is promised to us in Romans 8. A future that is pain free, suffering free, death free, and sin free. We hope for the moment when God will wipe away every tear and we will be home at last. Nothing we could endure in this life can be weighed against the glory of that day when we will see our Savior face to face.

Whatever the future holds,
God is good and His ways are perfect.
He is trustworthy and we are blessed.
Our hearts are filled with thankfulness.

I Need Thee Every Hour

Words by: *Annie Sherood Hawks. 1872*

©MichaelKravchuk.com

Music by: Robert Lowry

*D*o not fear, for I am with you;
  do not be afraid, for I am your God.
 I will strengthen you, I will also help you,
I will uphold you with my righteous right hand.

Isaiah 41:10

Confession

Emily Curtis

The world spins around me in a dizzying fury
Demanding my time and attention,
I worry that my all isn't enough and my best is left wanting.
Even as I lie to rest, I feel weighed down with haunting thoughts of failure,
Of things done all wrong, and I hear a faint dissonance in my heart's aching song.

Gasping for breath to sing one more note,
I feel unable to play the very music I wrote to encourage the hurting
And help them find rest.
I can't seem to shake this pain in my chest.

So I wave my white flag and surrender my sorrow.
I cry out in anguish with a voice weak and hollow.
"God in the heavens, the maker of man,
Do you see tears shed in darkness, or my cold, shaking hands
As I raise them to praise You and confess all my sins?

You are holy
holy
holy
Amen."

Then whispered to my heart with a melody clear
Was a promise from heaven and command not to fear
The plights in this life, no matter how the storm rages.
You will make all things beautiful as You compose all the pages
Of the glorious work only You could write,
And You'll never leave me alone in the night.

So now, though the darkness may at times still surround,
Where once there was panic,
Unspeakable peace now is found.

Peace I leave you, My peace I give you; not as the world gives, do I give to you.
Do not let your heart be troubled, nor let it be fearful.

John 14:27

Hope for the Languished Heart

Brighton (Lang) Hart

It is hard for me to know where to begin. I could start when I was a little girl and all I ever wanted was to be a wife and mother. I could start with how I had hoped that in college, I would find the man of my dreams and get married by 20. I could even start after college when I went mini-golfing and my date was the opposite of what I was looking for.

However, I think I will begin in the summer of 2015. I had just finished teaching a five-day music camp with my best friend. I came home and lamented to my mom, for probably the millionth time, that I just wished the right guy would come along. She gently asked me if I'd thought about online dating again. I had previously tried online Christian dating sites. She even offered to pay for it for a few months. I told her I'd try one more time.

The next day, on July 24, 2015, within a few hours of signing up, a really cute guy named Adam from Ohio wrote me a message. I instantly took a liking to him, and pretty soon we were writing long emails to each other multiple times a day. Then we were talking via Face Time on a daily basis. After asking my parents' permission to date me, Adam and I met for the first time in person on September 19, 2015. We had our first date at Disneyland where, right before the fireworks, he asked me to be his girlfriend. It was truly magical! From there, we dated long distance, visiting each other back and forth from California to Ohio.

In February of 2016, Adam made the bold decision to move to California! He drove 2,400 miles over three days with everything he owned packed up into his little white car. In March, while on a date at the Griffith Observatory atop the hills of Los Angeles, with a view of the Hollywood sign, Adam dropped to one knee and proposed marriage. It was so romantic—finally, all my dreams were coming true!

It was a whirlwind after that—finding my dress, putting together the little details. On August 6, 2016, I married Adam Richard Lang. It was the most blissful, lovely day. We honeymooned at Disneyland, then began making our home together. As each day passed, we fell more and more in love.

Adam had a night job and was typically home from work at around 2:00 a.m. Early in the morning of September 9, 2016, I had woken up about an hour after he was supposed to be home, wondering where he was. I texted him—no answer. I then called him; his phone went straight to voicemail. I figured his phone had died like it often did and decided to just wait up for him. Maybe he had to work late that night. I waited and waited. After thirty minutes, he still wasn't home. At that point, I talked with my mom and told her Adam wasn't home. She tried to calm me down and told me to wait a few more minutes before going to his work to look for him.

After another thirty minutes, I got in my car and headed to his work. It was still dark out, and I came upon an accident where there were police everywhere. I couldn't get past the wreck and there were too many officers around for me to really see anything. At the time, I truly didn't think it had anything to do with Adam; maybe that was God protecting me, I don't know. I took an alternate route to his work and didn't see his car. Everyone inside the building said he had left work on time. I feared the worst now. After searching the area and still not finding him, I didn't know what to do. One of the elders of our church started helping me search. It didn't take long for him to call me. He had found Adam! He told me to come to the hospital, he said he was in the ICU. He said he would meet me there. I raced to the hospital, only stopping once to pull over and vomit. I prayed. I pleaded with God to save him. We could get through this! I could take care of him if he was permanently injured. I would love him no matter what!

When I arrived, the elder from my church was outside, holding a bag of Adam's clothes. I ran up to him and said, "Where is he? Is he okay?" He just looked at me and said, "Brighton, he didn't make it. I saw him, he's gone." I don't really remember much after this. Only that I kept hearing a sound come out of me that I had never heard before, a deep groan, a moaning of agony. My husband, my sweet Adam, was gone. I asked my pastor to pray, and I would have collapsed if he hadn't held me up with his arms.

On September 9, 2016, just four weeks and six days after we were married, after leaving his work at 1:15 a.m., Adam's car was struck by a substance-impaired driver going over one hundred miles an hour, who was being chased by police. He was quickly taken to a nearby hospital, and despite their efforts, a short while later, died.

From that point on, it was just details—contacting family, friends, making arrangements. Adam's body wasn't released by the coroner until almost two weeks after he died, and we laid him to rest on September 22, 2016.

It has been nearly four years, and I miss him still. I went through many different changes because of this trial. I still am. But one thing has always remained constant. I have never once doubted the love and faithfulness of my Savior. God knew the moment Adam was going to go Home. He knew that I was going to have to live my life without him. Even though I was broken, the Lord never allowed me to fully break. He was always there, comforting me, holding me when I felt so alone and empty. When I cried out in the months of sleepless nights, where all I wanted was just one more minute with Adam, He was there, listening and giving me SO. MUCH. GRACE.

I will not say that I didn't struggle with sin, that I was the perfect picture of Christ. I had anger toward the driver (and his family) that killed Adam, anger at God for allowing me to fall in love and get married, only to rip him away. I struggled with bitterness and hurt. I was not perfect, but oh, my Savior was! He was there, convicting me, showing me so much mercy. He gave me friends and family members to show me truth and my sin in such loving and gentle ways, never expecting perfection. My family, especially, gave me so much forbearance—seeing my sin, but choosing when the right time was to confront me in love. I am so grateful for my pastors and elders, as well. They counseled me so many times, often in the middle of the night or at a last-minute's notice. God knew exactly the people I needed.

Even though I struggled, I still strove to grow in Christlikeness. I always knew that God was getting so much glory from this. When I would search the Psalms for comfort, a few passages would always be a balm to my heart. Psalm 6: 6–10; Psalm 8; and James 1. If you ever have the opportunity, memorize those verses! They will be an amazing treasure in your heart. I would often recite those verses in the middle of the night when sleep wouldn't come, and I was anxious and so lonely.

Another way of worshiping that brought me joy and great comfort was singing! If you know me, you know that I love to sing, more than almost anything. Some of the greatest moments of my life are attached to songs. A few that helped me during my deepest moments of grief were The Lord Is My Salvation, In Christ Alone, and My Worth Is Not in What I Own, all by Keith and Kristyn Getty. The latter was actually a duet that Adam and I sang at our church for a ladies' tea. It was recorded on video and I treasure that memory.

Even though four years have passed, and the Lord has been so good to me in bringing me countless other blessings, my journey of grief isn't over, and it has lasting effects. I have anxiety that is sometimes crippling. I still get counseling from time to time and my amazing husband, Wade, points me to Christ on a daily basis. In late 2017, I reconnected with a friend. Remember that terrible miniature golf date? Well, that guy is now my husband! We started dating in November of 2017, and ever so gently, I fell in love with Wade Hart. He was so understanding, so forbearing, and he always reminded me that he would never try and replace Adam, that he would always be a part of our story. On April 28, 2018, we were married in a sweet ceremony of our closest friends and family. Since then, we've built a beautiful life together and on October 2, 2019, we welcomed our son, Weston Adam Hart, into our family. Through no planning of our own, he was born on Adam's birthday. What a beautiful picture of God's amazing grace, mercy, and faithfulness. Out of the ashes comes beauty.

For those wondering how to comfort a grieving person, I would first encourage you to pray! God knew that you would be in this person's life; ask Him to help you meet that person's specific needs as they grieve. Second, I would ask the person how you can help them, what do they need? Everyone grieves so differently and it's important that your friend can be honest with what they truly need, instead of what others think they need. I would encourage you to be very patient and forbearing. There is no timeline on grief; yes, it will fade over time. But that time varies, and you could have three months of great progress and then suddenly be in darkness again.

Having friends who are there for you in the ups and downs is so helpful! Keep reaching out, keep inviting them places, it makes those grieving still feel needed and wanted. Finally, and most importantly, don't be afraid to confront them in love. If you see that they are struggling with a particular sin, please show them gently that you only want them to glorify Christ. There will be times when it's best to let things go, but when it's the right time, the Lord will give you the right words to say. I have an even deeper relationship with some of my friends because they chose the hard thing and confronted me in love about my sin.

My life is far from perfect, and there are days where I still miss Adam so much it hurts, but I am doing better. Each day is one day closer to seeing him again in glory, and until then, I am so thankful for the amazing blessings of my family, my husband, and my son. To God be all the glory!

Brighton and Adam
shortly after their wedding ~ 2016

Adam Richard Lang
October 2, 1987 ~ September 9, 2016

Brighton and Wade Hart
with Weston and Avonlea

Even though I was broken,
the Lord never allowed me to fully break.
He was always there,
comforting me, holding me.

HOPE & HELPS

Scripture I clung to on the hardest days/nights:
I searched the Psalms for comfort; a few passages would always be a balm to my heart. Psalm 6: 6–10; Psalm 8; and James 1. I also loved reading through the gospels, particularly John, to find hope in the gospel and Adam's security in Christ in Heaven.

Helpful ways people ministered to me:
- Sweet gifts of encouragement: notebooks to write my thoughts, and my favorite teas or snacks.

- Two of the most thoughtful gifts I received were a package of beautifully laminated Scriptures from a sweet friend who has since gone to heaven, and a gorgeous necklace that had meaningful charms inside representing Adam's life.

What you should NOT say to someone in a similar circumstance:
I would encourage anyone who is walking alongside a grieving person to remember that they may handle grief differently than you do. Don't tell them how they should be grieving. Don't assume that because they aren't talking about it, that they're "better." One of the most hurtful things was having people assume I was ready for things I wasn't. Like dating or visiting his grave. Just be kind and ask before assuming.

Hymns or songs that comforted me:
- *The Lord Is My Salvation*, Shane and Shane

- *In Christ Alone*, Keith and Kristen Getty

- *My Worth Is Not in What I Own*, Keith and Kristyn Getty

- *As the Deer*, Martin Nystrom

- *Great Is Thy Faithfulness*, Thomas Chisholm

- *O, the Deep Deep Love of Jesus*, Samuel Trevor Franc

The hope Jesus has given me through my loss of Adam:
My greatest hope is knowing I'll see Adam again. That he's no longer in pain and that all his worries are gone. I also have great hope that this trial will bring others to Christ. I have had hundreds of people pray for me, hundreds who know Adam's story, his coworkers even heard the gospel at his funeral. If even ONE person can be saved from hell, that's enough for me to suffer here on earth. That's what Adam would have wanted for his own life, and it's something I try to remember on the darkest days of my grief.

Hope for the Languished Heart

GREAT IS THY FAITHFULNESS

Thomas Chisholm   William M. Runyan

For I am convinced that neither death nor life,
neither angels nor demons,
neither the present nor the future
nor any powers, neither height nor depth,
nor anything else in all creation,
will be able to separate us
from the love of God that is in
Christ Jesus our Lord.

Romans 8:38-39

Sight

Emily Curtis

Stammering in blackest night,
Bruised, distraught and frightened,
Searching in the darkness for my eyes to be enlightened.
With trembling voice and weary knees,
I call to Adonai,
And in my spirit, deeply long,
For faith to become sight.

El Roi, the God who sees all things,
Who knows my every pondering,
Has sought me in the valley,
And shepherds me from wandering.

He binds my heart up tight to His,
El Kana, is His name.
He jealously protects me and guards me as His claim.

Jehovah, my God, my Rescuer,
Guide me as the Light,
'Til grief gives way to glory,
And faith gives way to sight.

For now we see in a mirror dimly,
but then face to face; now I know in part, but then
I will know fully, just as I have been fully known.

1 Corinthians 13:12

BY GRACE ALONE:
FROM BETRAYED WIFE
TO FULL-TIME CAREGIVER

LYNN WHITFORD[*]

We have been through so many real difficulties over the years of our marriage. I've had an autoimmune disease since I was a young child, so I've never had a day without pain. Two of our babies died from different causes, the same days they were born almost one year apart. We lost our home in a fire, and an earthquake damaged another home. My husband's job included weeks and sometimes months away from home. All these events were hard to go through, but the Lord gave us grace and strength to carry on.

On the hardest day of my life, I learned that my Christian husband, Franklin, had secretly been committing adultery for many years. He was not repentant, and neither was the other woman. After the initial shock settled down, and my tears stopped their continuous flow, I decided to fight for our marriage and not walk away. I wanted to keep my part of our marriage vows before God—in sickness and in health, for richer or poorer, for better or worse. I cried and asked the Lord to break my husband's, heart over his sin, and to please allow me to help him find his way back to Christ. Two friends joined me in this prayer.

For many weeks after learning about the adultery, I cried as I searched my Bible and studied the Scriptures, trying to understand what the Bible actually said about forgiveness, adultery, and marriage. I took pages and pages of notes, I prayed and prayed and re-read the Bible passages, listened to sermons, read books, and asked the Lord to help me understand what to do in a way that would honor Him.

I read in Proverbs (especially chapters 5, 6, and 7) about the sins of the adulteress and the adulterer, and how this sin gets started. I read that God chooses not to remember our sins, but as humans we don't have the ability to just forget like God does. (Isaiah 43:25) We need to forgive even while remembering what happened. We sometimes need to forgive the same offense over and over; every time we dwell on it or it comes to our minds (Matthew 18:21–22). We need to forgive for our own walk with the Lord. We forgive as Christ forgave us—unconditionally (Ephesians 4:32). Forgiving does not erase the sin—the sin still has consequences but forgiving makes our own hearts right with the Lord.

I read that adultery gives the option of divorce, even though God hates divorce (Malachi 2:16; Matthew 19:9; Luke 16:18; 1 Corinthians 6:18), and that divorce is never commanded or recommended in the Scriptures. I made the difficult choice to fight for my marriage, give my husband time to repent, and to keep my marriage vows. Most of my family and friends did not understand my choice to stay, but it was what God laid on my heart and I wanted to try to live for the Lord by keeping my marriage vows in spite of the circumstances.

I read in Ephesians 5:33 that it was my responsibility to respect my husband, even when it was extremely difficult to find something to respect. I had to be creative to think of ways to show him respect because that was my responsibility before God.

I read 1 Peter 3:1–4 where it says to live quietly before a disobedient husband. To me, this verse meant that it was not my job to remind Franklin of his sin and to nag him about it. He was responsible before God for his own choices, and I was responsible for my choices. I had to work hard to stay focused on respecting my husband and not nagging him about the sin he had chosen to do. After several years in a very difficult marriage, my husband told me that he stayed with me because of the way I had been living before him. The Lord was working and answering my prayers!

The Lord slowly worked in my husband's heart until he repented, and our marriage was finally beginning to heal, but the Lord changed our story in a different and unexpected way. Over the next five years, my husband suffered a brain injury from a fall, a heart attack that required surgeries, a serious debilitating stroke, and more that gave him many weeks in the hospital.

As I was recovering from a surgery myself, I was abruptly thrust into the role of being Franklin's full-time caregiver. It was suddenly up to me to wash his face and comb his hair, help him in the rest room, dress him, help him eat, help him remember and pronounce words, drive him and push his wheelchair to his many doctor and therapy appointments, and to be his medical advocate. While all this was happening to my husband, I had four more surgeries and recovery times for myself. Every day was completely full of physical, emotional, and financial challenges.

The challenges of the brain injuries from Franklin's fall and then his stroke were added to the adultery and forgiveness picture. With the most serious stroke, my husband lost the use of his dominant hand, lost his balance, his ability to stand and walk, his ability to care for himself, his ability to remember words, to swallow without choking, lost his ability to write, lost his short-term memory. He had huge outbursts of anger with no memory of it an hour later, and he lost the ability to make good decisions. He could not work, so our income was affected. We had to hire a caregiver to help for a few hours a day for the first few months. We remodeled parts of our home to make it wheelchair accessible. Therapists worked with him for several hours a day in the hospital, and when he was able to come home, the therapists came to our home to work with him to help him make new connections to the past information stored in his brain. When the therapists left each day after working with him and teaching me what to do, it was my responsibility to work with him for several more hours every day and continue working on each thing he was being taught to do again in extremely tiny increments.

Being a full-time, twenty-four-hours-a-day caregiver for a brain-injured person is not all joy. It is hard. Outbursts of anger and yelling are common. Inability to remember and do ordinary everyday things are common. His needs are constant and real, day and night. Meals still need to be cooked, laundry has to be done, groceries and supplies have to be ordered for delivery as much as possible, house cleaning still has to be done. It is an exhausting schedule! I cry almost every day just because I am so weary.

When a spouse suffers from a brain injury or stroke, you suddenly lose your own support system. You can no longer go to your mate for a much-needed comforting hug while you cry on his shoulder, even though he is sitting nearby. You lose your financial security because he is no longer able to physically or mentally work and provide. You lose friends because you can no longer do things for them or go places with them. You lose your church because his health is fragile, and he does not have self-control or stamina to go out in public. You are suddenly consumed with his full-time care, day and night, and trying to get a little rest for yourself. You become isolated because you have no other choice. The Lord sure chose a unique way to stretch me once again!

In all honesty, I cry a lot. I cry almost every day because I am so weary, and I am mourning the marriage that I had wished for. At the same time, I am blessed every time my husband of several decades reaches out his shaky hand for my hand and he tells me he loves me or thanks me for taking care of him. I am blessed with dear, understanding friends that have sent us gifts of meals and money when we were most in need. Once in a while, a card comes in the mail from an unexpected friend, sometimes with an enclosed check that will just cover a true need! First Peter 5:7 says, "He cares for you," and yes, HE really does care for our every need and HE cares about our hearts too!

I have blessings in serving my husband because "This is the day the Lord has made [for me!]; we will rejoice and be glad in it" (Psalm 118:24). This is what the Lord has chosen for me in this season of our lives.

I have the blessing of answered prayers and strength for each day. "In the day when I cried Thou did answer me, and strengthened me with strength in my soul" (Psalm 138:3). Every day I need God's strength to do what I have been called to do for my husband, and HE is always faithful to give me just enough strength for these tasks.

The Lord is working hard to fine-tune me for His glory! My strength often falters, but God's grace and His strength never falter.

Holding hands

*Lynn and Franklin holding hands while she recovers
from surgery and he recovers from his stroke.*

I have the blessing of answered prayers
and strength for each day.

HOPE & HELPS

It is the Lord who goes before you. He will be with you; He will not leave you or forsake you. Do not fear or be dismayed.—Deuteronomy 31:8

Scripture I clung to on the hardest days/nights:
In the day when I cried, Thou answered me, and strengthened me with strength in my soul.—Psalm 138:3.

Helpful ways people ministered to me:
- Meals or gift cards
- Cleaning
- Monetary gifts
- Flowers

What you should NOT say to someone in a similar circumstance:
It could have been worse!

Hymns or songs that comforted me:
- *All Your Anxieties, All Your Cares*, Edward H. Joy
- *Near to the Heart of God*, Cleland E. McAfee

The hope Jesus has given me through my suffering:
My strength often falters due to physical and mental exhaustion, but God's grace never falters. I have been encouraged by 2 Thessalonians 2:16 and these truths about grace:

GRACE: God's unmerited favor; a gift. Enabling power and spiritual healing offered through the mercy and love of Jesus Christ.

By Grace Alone

COME YE DISCONSOLATE

Come, ye dis - con - so - late, wher - e'er ye lan - guish,
Joy of the des - o - late, light of the stray - ing,
Here see the bread of life, see wa - ters flow - ing

Come to the mer - cy seat, fer - vent - ly kneel.
Hope of the pen - i - tent, fade - less and pure!
Forth from the throne of God, pure from a - bove.

Here bring your wound - ed hearts, here tell your an - guish;
Here speaks the Com - fort - er, ten - der - ly say - ing,
Come to the feast of love; come, ev - er know - ing

Earth has no sor - row that heav'n can - not heal.
"Earth has no sor - row that heav'n can - not cure."
Earth has no sor - row but heav'n can re - move.

Thomas Moore

Samuel Webbe

*O*n the day I called, You answered me;
  You made me bold with strength in my soul.
All the kings of the earth will give thanks to You,
O Lord, when they have heard the words of Your mouth.
  And they will sing of the ways of the Lord.
For though the Lord is exalted, yet He regards the lowly,
  but the haughty He knows from afar.
Though I walk in the midst of trouble, You will revive me;
  And Your right hand will save me.
The Lord will accomplish what concerns me;
  Your lovingkindness, O Lord, is everlasting;
  Do not forsake the works of Your hands.

Psalm 138:3–8

Cry For Mercy

Emily Curtis

———————

Oh how I long for this pain to cease,
For fear to fade and faith increase.

Restore to me my joy, O Lord,
For I am weak and oft' forlorn.
Strengthen the bones that you have made,
Make my voice steady to give you praise.

Focus my mind on the Truth of your Scripture.
Take captive my thoughts so my my life may be richer.
How I long to feel the depths of your peace,
To be assured of the grace you afforded to me.

Though I am frail, unsteady and weak,
Your promises hold fast for those who earnestly seek
To know You as You've made Yourself known,
To cling to Christ and call Heaven "home".

So as a compassionate father looks down on his child,
Cradle me now in arms meek and mild.
Show tender mercy as tears stream down my face,
And wrap me in unfathomable grace.

Remind me that I am fully known,
And bring to my thoughts all past mercies shown.
Precious Savior, bestow deep rest on my soul,
For even in my brokenness, in You I'm made whole.

Let us then with confidence draw near to the throne of grace,
that we may receive mercy and find grace to help in time of need.

———

Hebrews 4:16

HUDSON AND THE HOPE OF HEAVEN

CATHERINE BELL

It was a Thursday and it started out like any other summer day. Kevin went off to work and the boys and I started with our normal morning tasks. About mid-morning, we were heading out the door to make a quick visit to see some friends, but Hudson sat at the top of the stairs leading down to our basement garage and told me he couldn't come down the stairs. I asked him what he meant and then walked up to him to see if something was the matter.

Having assessed that he seemed fine other than being a little tired, I thought he might be coming down with a little summer cold of some sort and so decided we'd skip the visit to see friends. I had Hudson lay down to rest and phoned Kevin to give him a quick update. He said he'd come home for lunch just to check in. By lunchtime, Hudson wasn't improved and wasn't hungry, so Kevin suggested we call the pediatrician to see if we could get an appointment that afternoon, just to be cautious. We couldn't get in to see the doctor until later in the afternoon, so Kevin said he'd wrap up his work and come back home early to stay with Fisher while I took Hudson to the doctor's appointment.

After lunch, I brought Hudson downstairs to rest more in the master bedroom. I could keep a closer eye on him and we wouldn't disturb Fisher's nap that way. While he rested, I noticed that his breathing was becoming a little labored. It wasn't dramatic enough for me to think it was an emergency, and we had the doctor's appointment in just a couple of hours, so I just kept letting him rest. About an hour later, he woke up and called out for me. I went in to him, hearing that his breathing had become more labored and asked him to sit up to drink some water. But he said, "Mommy, I can't sit up." And he couldn't. His body had gone limp as a ragdoll.

I immediately called Kevin to tell him we needed to take Hudson to the doctor right then. He was already almost home by that time, and when he arrived a few minutes later, he took one look at Hudson and told me he was taking him directly to the emergency room. We called Kevin's dad to come over and stay with Fisher so I could follow Kevin and Hudson to the hospital.

It seemed like it took forever for my father-in-law to arrive, even though it didn't. I threw some clothes and toothbrushes in a duffle bag and grabbed Hudson's favorite stuffed bear and a few of his favorite books. When my father-in-law arrived, I remember saying something to assure him (but in reality, to assure myself) that everything would be fine. I kissed Fisher and headed to the hospital, which was a 20-minute drive away.

Not long after, Kevin called me from the hospital. He said, "I don't want you to get pulled over or get in a crash, but you need to hurry." That was the first moment I really understood that something was seriously wrong with Hudson.

What I didn't know was that just before that moment, Hudson had become unresponsive in the ER of the hospital. The doctors had been giving him oxygen and were running all sorts of tests to try and figure out what might be going on with his little body, but all of a sudden, his heart stopped beating.

When I arrived at the hospital a few minutes later, Kevin told me what was happening.

It was a whirlwind of news and then a rush to the room where what seemed like an army of doctors and nurses were all over Hudson giving him CPR, watching monitors, running tests, and giving medicines. The lead ER doctor took us to a side room and explained what was happening and that they were trying to stabilize Hudson enough to connect him to ECMO, a bypass-type machine that would keep his heart functioning and give the doctors time to figure out what was wrong. He told us that Hudson's symptoms presented so rapidly and randomly that they didn't yet know how to treat him.

God allowed Hudson's body to stabilize enough for ECMO and so we moved from the ER to PICU (pediatric intensive care unit), where a new team of doctors and specialists continued the work of figuring out what was making Hudson sick, and hopefully find a successful treatment. But, over the next 36 hours, no tests, scans, or cultures yielded any clue to the doctors as to what was wrong with Hudson. His symptoms didn't fit any known infection, reaction, disease, or genetic condition. Slowly, his kidneys began to fail and circulation problems developed in his legs. His little body became distorted and cold. As time went on, repeated EEGs showed Hudson's brain had ceased to function.

All during this time in the hospital, we were surrounded with close friends and family. Their prayers and presence were part of God's sustaining grace in those long two days. Two dear friends were physicians practicing at that hospital and were able to give us counsel from both a biblical and medical perspective. It was impossibly difficult to see our sweet boy in such a state of physical decay, but we spent the hours reading his favorite books and Bible to him, talking to him, and reminding him of how much God loved him and we loved him.

Finally, with no positive reaction to any treatment given him, and increasing evidence that his body systems had ceased functioning on their own, it became apparent to us that Hudson's life on earth had ended. When the life-support systems were stopped, his heart stopped beating and he didn't breathe on his own. We saw this as a mercy from God, who made it so very clear that while Hudson's body had died, he was now fully alive in the presence of Jesus Christ.

Both of us had an immediate sense of comfort and peace that can only be attributed to the Holy Spirit. The Comforter had been with us those past two days and now we felt a very real assurance that He would be there every day in the future. It's because of this assurance that we were able to comfort others around us and tell them truthfully that everything would be okay.

But, of course, we also felt the strong and natural human emotions you would expect. We left the hospital that Saturday evening in a surreal daze. Hudson had been with us nearly every day of his life and now he wasn't ever going to be there again. There was a gaping hole in our hearts that was represented visibly by his empty car seat on that ride home.

Forefront in our minds was how we would share the news with Fisher. You see, Fisher and Hudson were always together. They were the best of buddies. Even though Fisher was only two years old at the time, we knew that he would quickly notice his big brother wasn't around. As we were putting Fisher to bed that night, he finally asked, "Where's Hudson?" Even this heartbreaking moment, which was impossibly difficult to navigate in our own strength, was made easy by God's grace. Fisher was satisfied with the simple, yet completely truthful answer, "Hudson isn't here. He's with Jesus."

As early as that evening, we both agreed that we wanted to continue talking about Hudson in normal daily conversation and to keep pictures of him around the house. As hard as it was to talk of Hudson in the first weeks and months without him, we always wanted Fisher to feel comfortable asking and talking about him. We also knew that this would be a repeated opportunity for instructing Fisher about the nature of life in a fallen world and the exclusive and ultimate hope we can have in Christ to make all things right. As time went on, we always honestly explained to Fisher the things that happened to Hudson and answered his questions as transparently as we could. He has always been fine with our answers, accepting them fully with the faith of a child.

Over the years, we have seen that most of what Fisher remembers of Hudson are actually stories we have told him about when they were little together. But we still chose to give those memories to him. We made a photo book for him full of snapshots of just the two of them together, with captions explaining all the fun they enjoyed as well as a few scriptures to point him to the reality that through Christ, he can see Hudson again in heaven one day.

As we walked through the days after Hudson died, we experienced a very real sense of being carried along by our heavenly Father. We were sustained by prayer and the truth of Scripture we already knew, coming to understand more fully the truth that God's love ordains all things for believers so that we might grow in our love for Him and dependence on Him. In other words, "for those who love God, he causes all things to work together for good, for those who are called according to his purpose" (Romans 8:28–29).

Kevin and I also came to see more clearly how the church—the Body of Christ—works. Our church family visited, called, brought food, played with Fisher, watered our large vegetable garden, and mowed our yard. We received wonderful pastoral care from our elders as we planned for Hudson's memorial service and burial. Their open and sincere counsel confirmed our desire to have Hudson's body buried in a cemetery so that we could continue to have that physical place as a teaching object for our family and friends—a picture of the sure hope of a coming bodily resurrection. Our pastors gladly arranged the memorial service so that it would be focused on calling people to repentance and faith in Christ, since so many of our family members and Kevin's work colleagues were unbelievers. In fact, the care our church family showed us was a distinct witness to many unbelievers of something they lacked, and this led to opportunities for us to share the importance of being members of a solid, Bible-teaching church.

Even more than that, we were given so many opportunities to share the reason for our own hope and peace through the gospel of Jesus Christ. These moments began to happen even while Hudson was being treated in the hospital. Doctors, nurses, colleagues, family members, and friends seemed to marvel at how anyone could have peace at a time like that. In these interactions, we recognized that God had fulfilled one of our earnest prayers for Hudson. We used to pray that God would use him to spread the gospel, perhaps as a missionary one day. We named him Hudson after Hudson Taylor, a pioneering missionary to China in the 1800s. We began to see that through Hudson's death, God fulfilled those prayers fully, even if it wasn't in the way we expected.

One aspect of Hudson's death is particularly hard for many people to hear about: we still do not have a medical explanation for what happened. The pathologist who conducted his autopsy listed a heart-related nominal cause of death but acknowledged that there was surely some other unidentified root issue to blame. In their efforts to pinpoint the true cause of death, the PICU team of specialists worked with Hudson's pediatrician and additional specialists from prestigious hospitals around the country, comparing his case to other rare cases. This went on for a whole year, yet every test came back negative, and every known condition was ruled out. So, scientifically, his death remains a mystery.

But we have great hope even in this mystery because of what David writes in Psalm 139:16: "In your book were written, every one of them, the days that were formed for me, when as yet there was none of them." David declares that God chooses the length of our lives even before we are conceived in our mother's womb. So, we say with David, "in your book were written, every one of them, the days that were formed for Hudson." This was a great source of comfort as we watched Fisher grow, and as the Lord gave us more children. He gave us two more boys as a matter of fact, one of whom has the middle name, Hudson.

In all of this, Kevin and I gained a greater sense of eternity that affects every aspect of our daily lives. Certainly, this includes profound gratitude that God has chosen to secure Hudson in heaven and that we will never have to think of him suffering on this earth. For this reason, we have an even greater and more personal anticipation of heaven ourselves, and a sharper focus upon the hope we have in Christ—a hope that transcends the difficulties of this life. Perhaps most practically, we realize the true brevity of life and the futility of chasing earthly treasures. Rather, we realize that by God's grace, we are already built on the immovable rock of Christ who is a sure and steadfast anchor of our souls (Hebrews 6:19).

Kevin, Catherine, Hudson,
and Fisher Bell ~ 2011

Hudson Jude Bell
May 22, 2009 ~ August 10, 2013

We were sustained by prayer
and the truth of Scripture we already knew,
coming to understand more fully
the truth that God's love ordains all things
for believers so that we might grow
in our love for Him and dependence on Him.

HOPE & HELPS

Oh, the depth of the riches and wisdom and knowledge of God! How unsearchable are his judgments and how inscrutable His ways! For who has known the mind of the Lord, or who has been His counselor? Or who has given a gift to Him that he might be repaid? For from Him and through Him and to Him are all things. To Him be glory forever. Amen.
—Romans 11:33-36

Scripture we clung to on the hardest days/nights:
Psalm 18:30; 33:20–22; 68:19–20; Isaiah 42:3; John 16:33; Romans 11:33–36; Philippians 3:20–21; Colossians 3:15; 1 Thessalonians 4:13; 1 Peter 5:7

Helpful ways people ministered to us:
- Meals brought every night for several weeks. At the beginning, this was hugely helpful. We were planning a funeral and were exhausted. By the end, we didn't feel like we "needed" this as much, so we invited several families to stay and eat with us, providing some wonderful fellowship.

- Friends kept inviting us to participate in normal activities. Even when we said no, they didn't stop asking. This was a reminder to us that others were continuing to pray and think of us even when we weren't as involved as usual.

- People shared what they loved about Hudson or some special memory they had. They told us they missed him (and actually still do even years later).

- A close friend who happens to be an "older woman" (Titus 2:3–5) came to talk with me every few weeks for several months after Hudson died. Mostly she just wanted to sit and listen to how I was doing. Sometimes she'd share a book or a passage that she thought might help me. Sometimes she'd ask if I wanted practical help with a difficult task, like putting Hudson's clothes away. Her faithfulness to pray for me and take time to visit consistently was such a blessing.

What you should NOT say to someone in a similar circumstance:
- Saying/doing nothing, as if nothing happened.

- Give advice about how practicalities or grief should be dealt with (e.g., "just get busy and time passing will make it better").

- Quote scripture or Christian platitudes as if one single thought will make it better. "I'm so sorry" is a much better salve on a wounded heart.

Hymns or songs that comforted us:
- *My Heart Is Filled with Thankfulness*, Keith and Kristyn Getty
- *He Will Hold Me Fast*, Keith and Kristyn Getty and Matt Merker
- *I Asked the Lord That I Might Grow*, John Newton
- *The Perfect Wisdom of Our God*, Keith and KristynGetty

- *More Love to Thee*, Elisabeth Prentiss

The hope that Jesus has given us through our loss of Hudson:

As we consider the uncertainties of life here on earth, we necessarily take comfort in the certain hope of salvation through Jesus Christ. We have great hope for Hudson's eternity, and our own, because of Christ. Not only that, but we have great hope for every moment of this life because our eternal security in Christ has already begun. So, every circumstance we encounter is perfectly designed by God for our good, so that He might be glorified in us. No matter what may still happen during the 70-80 years God may grant us (Psalm 90:10), it is good and it is a part of what God has designed to make us more like Christ. That is an incredible gift! And it also serves as a reminder of the kindness of God. So often in this life, we don't face severe trials. We live life from day to day as if these peaceful times are beyond anything we deserve. But even in the trials, God is there. He knows exactly what we face because He designed it (2 Cor. 12:8–9). He cares for us in the midst of the trial (Psalm 23:4). And He will not let us go (Rom. 8:35–39; Phil. 1:6).

Every circumstance we encounter is perfectly designed by God for our good, so that He might be glorified in us.

What Wondrous Love Is This

*B*ut we do not want you to be uninformed, brothers and sisters,
about those who are asleep, so that you will not grieve
as indeed the rest of mankind do, who have no hope.
For if we believe that Jesus died and rose from the dead,
so also God will bring with Him those who have fallen asleep through Jesus.
For we say this to you by the word of the Lord,
that we who are alive and remain until the coming of the Lord
will not precede those who have fallen asleep.
For the Lord Himself will descend from heaven with a shout,
with the voice of the archangel and with the trumpet of God,
and the dead in Christ will rise first.
Then we who are alive, who remain,
will be caught up together with them in the clouds
to meet the Lord in the air, and so we will always be with the Lord.
Therefore, comfort one another with these words.

1 Thessalonians 4:13-18

Precious Boy

Emily Curtis

Once there was a boy, precious as could be,
He loved to learn and laugh and smile
And dance and read and sing.
He loved his family very much
And had friends near and far.
Everyone who knew him, held him in their heart.

You see, this boy was special in oh so many ways,
He observed the world around him,
Grasped things beyond his age.
He had a tender heart,
And loved the Lord above.
He loved to hear the stories of the awesome things He's done.
His hugs could melt a heart of stone,
And his smile made your day.
Indeed, this child was special in every single way.

With tear-filled prayers we begged the Lord
To leave this little boy,
Down here on earth to grow and flourish
And bring us daily joy.
We prayed the Lord would strengthen Him
And make him whole again.
We did not know He would answer prayer
By perfecting him in Heaven.

To God be the glory, great things He has done,
Through this beautiful child
Who was friend, brother, and son.
What a blessing it has been to us to see God write his story,
And know that in the final chapter He brought about God's glory.
To Jesus be the praise for all life great and small,
And may we trust the sweetest name,
Who holds the dearest boy of all.

NEVER LOSE HOPE

DAISY COX

*Suffering produces endurance … endurance produces character
… character produces hope.*—Romans 5:3–4 (ESV)

These are words to a verse I never knew I would have to cling to so tightly and be blessed to understand so intimately by the love of my life, my Lord and Savior—Jesus Christ.

It was my birthday, July 23, 2012. I was scheduled to have my 20-week ultrasound. My husband made our family omelets for breakfast and my two precious daughters joyfully loaded into the car, excited to hear their sister's or brother's heart beat! Finally, after two miscarriages, my baby had made it to 20 weeks. My heart was so excited to hear that heart beat! You could not wipe the smile off our faces! We all descended upon that ultrasound room with anticipation and joy. As the ultrasound tech began taking pictures, the Lord stirred in my heart a sense of concern. She told us that she was going to grab the doctor to come in and look at the photos with us.

Immediately I knew something was wrong, very wrong, and as I lay there I told my husband, John, something was not right. As he held our daughters in his strong arms he looked in my eyes and said, "What? What do you mean?" And then … the doctor came in and began the ultrasound. As he took photos, he kindly and quietly told us there was no heartbeat. Before the last syllable came out of his mouth a wave of God's amazing grace washed over me. Three things came to mind. God loves me. He hasn't forgotten me. He's going to see me through this. My daughters were in the room, they were ages 5 and 2. We all wept. My husband sweetly took the girls from the room and I spoke with the doctor alone.

As I spoke with the doctor, reality hit and I was processing being induced to deliver my baby who had died. As he described what I would have to walk through the next day the Lord brought to my mind, "we don't grieve as those without hope." I have hope I thought! I have hope in God! The doctor told me he was so sorry and he didn't have the words. I realized in that moment I had what I needed. I had Christ and the strength of almighty God on my side and I shared with him the verse and he stared at me stunned. I went home and God graciously planned for me to talk to a friend who had walked through a stillbirth and told me what to expect. This was so helpful and comforting, although the reality of it all was starting to weigh on my soul. The next day, on the way to the hospital, there was a glorious sunrise and I was reminded that God had ordained all of these days. He loves me.

The first thing my husband did when we got into the delivery room was ask for another ultrasound just to make sure there really was no heartbeat. Our doctor completely understood and we had an ultrasound that confirmed no heartbeat. I was put on medicine to begin the labor process and now we had to wait. Waiting was very hard. We had worship music on and we read through scripture but it was agony. We did find out that it was a girl! So, now we decided to name her. As we read through the verses in Romans 5 we decided on Hope Elizabeth. God then gave me a tremendous surprise, my nurse walked in; she was a believer I had met three weeks before! She had been praying for me all morning and she asked if she could play a song for me. She proceeded to play one of the best songs I have ever heard. It was called Our God Is in Control by Steven Curtis Chapman. The chorus of the song praises God for His holiness in the midst of unspeakable loss. I cried and realized this moment was a time of worship. In the hospital bed before delivering our precious Hope, we were standing on holy ground and the presence of God was palpable.

The time finally came for Hope's arrival! She was miraculously born in the sac and so she was preserved. The nurse cleaned her up and put her in a blanket for us. We got to hold her and John sang a lullaby over her. We held her for a while and prayed and cried. Then the hardest part came for me, to give her to the nurse. This was my baby, my beautiful gift from God. Why can I not take my baby home? How can I leave her with strangers? I didn't want to give her to them but I had to. And the Lord gave me the strength to walk out of the hospital with empty arms.

My nurse had just begun a ministry at the hospital to moms who had lost babies by making them a box, stamping the hand print and foot print if possible and taking photos for a small album. The day we drove home from the hospital a pastor called us and prayed for us. One thing he prayed over us was that God would show us one-thousand reasons why He took Hope home. That prayer gave me such faith and anticipation to keep track of those reasons and I began a journal listing the lessons, insights and reasons. To this day I update the journal and I am almost up to one thousand!

The following days were so hard. I remember crying and praying on my knees before the Lord, and He met me again and again. He illumined a path of praise in the darkness for me. I was able to sing to the Lord in the midst of the struggle. I rewrote the words to one of my favorite hymns, *Take My Life And Let It Be*:

Take her hands and let them move
At the impulse of Thy Love
Take her feet, and let them be
Swift and beautiful for Thee

Take her voice and let her sing
Always, only for You my King
Take her, she was meant to be
Ever, only all for Thee

From out of the mouth of babes
You have predetermined praise
And my precious little one, together
One day we will run
Into the Arms of the Eternal One

December 9, 2012, was my due date so we decided to go to the hospital and gave gifts to the next five delivering moms. The gift included a note with Hope's hand and foot print, the gospel message, a small Christmas book and candy cane. I wrote my testimony on a piece of paper and put the full gospel message on the back. I gave one to my doctor and basically everyone I knew. God has used Hope's little life in so many ways. The nurse who delivered Hope became the bereavement counselor at the hospital because of what we walked through. I had a checkup with my doctor and he told me, "I hope you don't mind but I've been passing out that flier to all of the delivering moms who have lost babies." I teared up and thought, does he realize he is passing out the GOSPEL! God will take any small act of faith and use it beyond what we can imagine. Hope really does get us to the finish line where we will see the Lord face to face. These trials, although weighty, are a light and momentary affliction compared to the eternal weight of glory God has stored up for those who love Him.

As I reflect on this trial from eight years ago I am blown away by the conversations, ministry opportunities, depth of comfort I have received from the Holy Spirit, and the strength God has built in my life from enduring this loss. He has held my hand every step of the way.

The Lord didn't stop there! He blessed me with a son two years later! In the delivery room there were some holy hallelujahs and tears of joy! My husband, John, had just been diagnosed with lymphoma cancer weeks before our due date. By God's grace, John was delcared "cured" in 2020!

If we could just see the waves of God's grace crashing into the depth of His ocean of love for us in these trials, then we can behold His glory in it all. Charles Spurgeon stated, "I have learned to kiss the wave that throws me against the Rock of Ages." Grace to stand and praise Him, grace to fall at His feet in worship. A friend helped me write a worship song that I still sing today, *Still I'll Praise You*:

> I can feel the rising waters
> Surrounding me here in the dark
> But I'm not alone I sense your presence
> Upholding me; remind me who You are
>
> You aren't taken aback
> You aren't caught off guard
> None of this surprises you
> And though I want a way around this
> You've shown me the only way is through
>
> (chorus)
> I will stay and face the dark
> If you're the light I'm headed to
> I will kiss the waves that crash down
> If they carry me to you
> No matter what
> You take me through
> Still I'll praise you

You walked the path of suffering
You could have fled and made the pain go away
But you stayed and faced the agony
Because you knew it was the only way

And one day you will wipe away each tear
And maybe you'll show me the reasons why
But for now I'm meant to stay right here
Oh, and make the most of this time

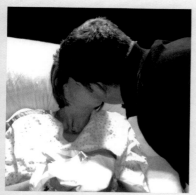

Daisy & John with their baby Hope

My Story of Hope

Today, December 9, 2012 would have been my due date with my sweet daughter, Hope. I went in for a 20 weeks ultrasound and there was just no heartbeat. I delivered her and she was so beautiful. Perfect hands and feet which the picture above shows and they are actual size. She measured 18 weeks. These moments in life leave us with many unanswered questions and challenge our beliefs and resolve. The truth is God has give me the perfect opportunity to share with you who my hope is, my beautiful Savior and Lord Jesus Christ. I want to share with you just how wonderful He is.

Peace with God Through Faith

"Therefore, since we have been justified by faith, we have peace with God through our Lord Jesus Christ. Through him we have also obtained access by faith into this grace in which we stand and we rejoice in hope of the glory of God. Not only that, but we rejoice in our sufferings, knowing that the suffering produces endurance, and endurance produces character, and character produces hope, and hope does not put us to shame, because God's love has been poured into our hearts through the Holy Spirit who has been given to us."
Romans 5:1-5

Hope Cox
December 9, 2012

HOPE & HELPS

Scripture we clung to on the hardest days/nights:
By day the Lord commands His steadfast love, and at night His song is with me. A prayer to the God of my life. –Psalm 42:8 (ESV)

Helpful ways people ministered to us:
- Gave me grace and space to grieve.
- Prayed and brought meals.
- Sent cards and books.
- One sweet friend actually walked me through the delivery process the day before so I was prepared. Upon her recommendation, we brought a blanket to the hospital with us and wrapped her up in it. Since we couldn't take our baby home, we took the blanket that held her home with us.

What you should NOT say to someone in a similar circumstance:
- That you know what it's like (if you've never experienced it).
- Don't say "I'm so sorry, I know when my dog died I was so sad." It was not an animal; it was a human being. Don't use pet loss to relate to child loss.

Hymns or songs that comforted us:
- *Unspeakable Joy,* Oceans
- *Still I'll Praise You*; this is the song that God wrote on my heart and I wrote down and sing often.

The hope Jesus has given me through my loss of my daughter, Hope:
Joni Eareckson Tada said, "Hope is like holding onto the thin string of a kite and if you would just let it, He has the power to LIFT you off the ground!" My daughter, Hope, is in heaven and I praise God for her brief life here on earth and her mark on eternity!

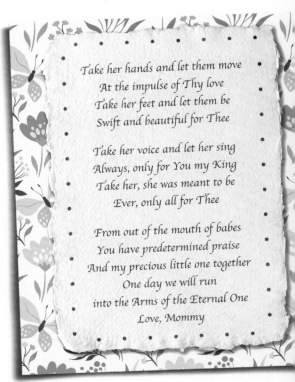

Take her hands and let them move
At the impulse of Thy love
Take her feet and let them be
Swift and beautiful for Thee

Take her voice and let her sing
Always, only for You my King
Take her, she was meant to be
Ever, only all for Thee

From out of the mouth of babes
You have predetermined praise
And my precious little one together
One day we will run
into the Arms of the Eternal One
Love, Mommy

Take My Life and Let It Be

Take my life__ and__ let it be / Con - se - crat - ed,__ Lord, to__Thee;
Take my hands and__ let them move / At the im - pulse of Thy__ love;
Take my voice and__ let me sing / Al - ways, on - ly,__ for my__King;
Take my sil - ver__ and my gold / Not a mite would I with-hold;
Take my will__ and__ make it Thine / It shall be__ no__ long-er__mine;
Take my love;__ my__ Lord, I pour / At Thy feet__ its__ trea sure__store;

Take my mo - ments and my days,__ / Let them flow in
Take my feet and__ let them be__ / Swift and beau - ti -
Take my lips and__ let them be__ / Filled with mes - sa -
Take my in - tel - lect and use__ / Ev - 'ry pow'r as
Take my heart it__ is Thine own,__ / It shall be Thy
Take my - self and__ I will be__ / Ev - er, on - ly,

cease - less__ praise,__ / Let them flow in__ cease - less praise.
ful__ for__ Thee,__ / Swift and beau - ti - ful for Thee.
ges__ from__ Thee,__ / Filled with mes - sa - ges from Thee.
Thou shalt__ choose, / Ev - 'ry pow'r as__ Thou shalt choose.
roy - al__ throne,__ / It shall be Thy__ roy - al throne.
all__ for__ Thee,__ / Ev - er, on - ly,__ all for Thee.

Frances R. Havergal

©MichaelKravchuk.com

H.A. Cesar Malan

*T*he Lord will send His goodness in the daytime;
and His song will be with me in the night,
a prayer to the God of my life.

———

Psalm 42:8

Hope

Emily Curtis

Friend,
Let me sit with you in the ashes & grieve with you in sorrow,
As your heart mourns the loss of all the dreams you held for tomorrow.
Cry upon My shoulder & let Me bear your pain,
Until your heart is strengthened so you can rise again.

And when the morning comes, please take My outstretched hand,
Look up at My face & find courage as you stand.

I will replace your tears with joy & give you grace & peace to cope,
And I will fill all your tomorrows with the sweetest gift of hope.

You are my hiding place and my shield; I hope in Your Word.

Psalm 119:114

SHE DANCES WITH JESUS

JOHN COX

I never thought I would know Christ's comfort as I lay crying on the floor of a hospital bathroom. I never thought I would be able to know Christ's peace as I sat in a chemo chair. I never thought as the greatest of suffering pressed down on my family, Christ's hope would flow more greatly than the tears that were shed. Yet this is a story designed by a sovereign God whose light shined in every dark moment, and the one who is redeeming every hardship. It is a story that brought me to the greatest point of desperation to reveal the very thing I needed was not a coping mechanism or temporal relief, it was a person, and His name is Jesus Christ. The Lord might be navigating you through your own story and the hurts are personal. And though there is not a person who can understand your trial, your destination of hope is the same as mine—Jesus Christ.

Now when I say Jesus, I am not speaking about the "mascot" of the Christian faith, but the master of our lives! He is not only the God who was, but the God who is! The God who right now is shining His life-giving light on the path before you and speaking His life-altering words to lift you.

"You make known to me the path of life; in your presence there is fullness of joy; at your right hand are pleasures forevermore" (Psalm 16:11). Jesus knows He is the one who can part the clouds of our spirit and the one who can wipe the tears from our face when it hurts from hours of mourning. That is why our stories are not simply about suffering, for every man suffers. Rather, our stories are those of endurance. Why? Suffering is the pain that can be pressed upon us, but endurance is the gift of God's supernatural strength to rise up under the greatest of challenges, in order to produce in us the greatest of hope.

As a pastor, I would like to tell you how I selflessly walked through these moments with poise and grace, confident in the Lord at every moment and in complete peace. But this is not Narnia; pain is real, and life is not a picnic! Rather, God took me to the depths of myself to show me the heights of who He is. He allowed me to feel like the space shuttle coming in for re-entry and the panels are flying off. And when you feel like you are only able to hold on by our fingernails, you know He is holding on to you.

This is my story of hope.

I will never forget the exhilaration of walking into the doctor's office at our 20-week appointment to see our daughter's ultrasound. After two miscarriages and two living daughters, we were thrilled to get our final ultrasound and see our daughter, Hope. We brought our girls this time to see, because the time before it was as if she was dancing in the womb! This was a time of rejoicing!

We crowded around mommy with excitement to see our little one, and then the color washed from the nurse's face. Her smile sank into her stomach and she left the room. Our doctor came in, sighed, and told us she was gone. We shuddered in disbelief and I pressed the doctor to look again but she was gone. We huddled together and cried; our Hope was gone.

The next day we made our way to the hospital to deliver our little Hope. As I watched my wife prepare for this I had no words. I sought to be an anchor for her, but as the weight crushed upon me I did not want her to see me this way. So I went into the bathroom, fell to the ground and wept bitterly. But it was in this place of desperation I met with my God. I prayed, "Lord, I can't do this." And He reminded me to be "casting all your anxieties on him, because he cares for you" (1 Peter 5:7). He reminded me, apart from Him I can do nothing (John 15:5), and it was only He who could lift the weight from my chest.

Then I prayed, "Lord, I don't know what to say." And He refreshed me, "Be still, and know that I am God" (Psalm 46:10). As a father and husband, I had no words to say to my bride as I had never walked this road before. Husbands and fathers, there are moments in your life you will not know what to say. I learned in the silence that He comforts us with His presence. The most heartening thing I learned was to simply sit with my wife and say nothing. There would be time for words, but now was the time for waiting. It is in these moments that we lead our brides into the quiet of His presence to experience His comfort and rest in the truth that He is working in the waiting. To know that as we wait to get through the trial, He is already at work to redeem our tragedy. A.W. Tozer said, "We need never shout across the spaces to an absent God. He is nearer than our own soul, closer than our most secret thoughts"

As His gift of endurance began to raise strength in our hearts, we knew this was not simply about us. For God is the one "who comforts us in all our affliction, so that we may be able to comfort those who are in any affliction, with the comfort with which we ourselves are comforted by God" (2 Corinthians 1:4).

The greatest partner I have in comforting others is my wife. We have waited and watched, and now stand back in amazement as we have been able to care for families who have faced desperate loss and share with them the power of God's redemption. There is a time, as Job, to sit in the ashes, but also a time to rise up and watch His plan unfold.

On Hope's birthday, we went to the hospital and passed out a track we made to everyone we saw. We had placed on it her handprints and footprints, our story, and the power of the gospel. Our unbelieving doctor to this day still gives it out to his patients. Our believing delivery nurse was so moved by watching God work in that room, she shifted her career to be on the front line every day with hurting families to show them Jesus, and still to this day Hope's testimony is impacting many. God is at work.

Remember this, parents, your child will have as much of an impact on your life as anyone! Though their life may be brief, it plays a significant part in His eternal plan. But may we not simply look for the reasons, but for the redemption. There is no weight of reasons I can find that can salve my mind at the loss of my daughter. Likewise, there are not enough reasons that can mount up to say it was worth God sending His Son to die. Rather, we know God's plan is that of redemption—to take the hardest day or the darkest of souls and breathe into them the life of heaven.

It is important that we remember and anchor our hearts to this truth, for our hearts can be tossed. The day after we had Hope, looked into her eyes, and held her little body, we went home, and I had no idea the anger that was to come. For the next six months the smallest irritation would set me off; I was short-fused, for I was heartbroken. There are moments where we must recognize the fragility of our flesh in order to lean hard into the strength of His promise! He is pouring down His immeasurable grace despite our weakness. This grace is the fuel for our endurance, for it fuels our adoration for Him! For when we drink of His Word and dwell in His presence, a longing for His grace abounds, and eternal satisfaction floods in.

How I wish this was the end of the story of endurance, and since those moments, could say I have lived in the plateaus of peace, and frolicked in fields of happiness! But all books have many chapters.

"And we all, with unveiled face, beholding the glory of the Lord, are being transformed into the same image from one degree of glory to another" (2 Corinthians 3:18).

In October of 2013, it was a time for joy: my wife was pregnant with my son, our girls were amazing, and ministry was thriving. It was in this moment that I was longing for His presence even more, so I went to my office, got on my knees, and cried out to the Lord, "Grow my faith!" He answered, and I got sick the next day. Several months later I was diagnosed with Hodgkin lymphoma.

After months of coughing and intense pain, the doctor called and said to me, "You have lymphoma." I had no clue what this meant so I asked, "What does that mean?" The doctor replied coldly, "What do you mean what does that mean? You have cancer, and another doctor will call you about survivability." Click. The phone went silent as my wife walked in the room pregnant. The thoughts: I will never see my son, I will not be here for my wife, were met with a truth just as quickly. But I know Jesus! I know He is a God who is there to comfort, there to guide, and has a redeeming plan. Did I like the plan? No! But did I trust my God? By His grace! Yes.

So, we did the first thing on our minds, we cried out to the Lord! And He answered. Within weeks I was poked in every way you can be, radioactive from tests so I could not be near my pregnant wife, and passed from doctor to doctor like a trading card. God heard our prayer, and He brought us to a great doctor who pursued us and spoke truth. I had a 5"x6" tumor in my chest amidst others, and he said, "I might be able to save your life." I was about a month away from seeing Jesus, so we got to work. The plans of chemotherapy and radiation were before me as if they were the answer of redeeming me from my plight. So, in Adriamycin, Bleomycin, Vinblastine, and Dacarbazine do I trust? "Some trust in chariots and some in horses, but we trust in the name of the Lord our God" (Psalm 20:7). This verse rang in my ear as I laid on the biopsy table. It was my God who can heal, it was my God who can care for my family more than I ever can, it was and is my God who is the Redeemer!

And so our new journey began. Well-meaning people came to care, and I quickly realized that, even as a pastor, I had been saying the wrong things! So we learned what not to say! (See notes at end of story.)

After a year of treatment, it has been five years of restoration. For every story of pain, there are more of His redemption. For we endure, not by our strength but His own. And we continue to endure. Trials come and though they may shift in category, they always lead to the same destination—Christ.

This is the hope we have! Not that our problems will be solved, our issues will go away, so we can finally live our life! But rather to know that every hardship and trial that comes our way is a gift from Him to declare His truth! To know that as the disciples in Acts 5:41—He considered us worthy to suffer for His sake. Why? So that others would see that the hope in Christ we have is not in temporal deliverance from pain, but eternal deliverance of sin!

We are living, breathing signposts that show the path to true hope in Christ. Peter said, "but in your hearts honor Christ the Lord as holy, always being prepared to make a defense to anyone who asks you for a reason for the hope that is in you; yet do it with gentleness and respect"(1 Peter 3:15). This means that when trials come and we are crushed, hope emerges, and when it does, it does not make sense to the world, and they will come and ask, "how can you have this amid the chaos?" Because of Jesus.

Our endurance sweats out the aroma of hope. When the sick sing, when the paralyzed praise, when those with a fatal diagnosis resound a faithful declaration, it reveals the object of their hope: Jesus.

This is the strength of our life, even when we don't feel like it. There are days where, like Jeremiah, we will feel, "My endurance has perished; so has my hope from the Lord (Lamentations 3:18). In such moments, may we speak God's truth against our feelings, "The steadfast love of the Lord never ceases; his mercies never come to an end; they are new every morning; great is your faithfulness 'The Lord is my portion,' says my soul, 'therefore I will hope in him' (Lamentations 3:22–24).

The birth of Jack Cox
2014

Living out
James 1:2—4

The Cox family.
2015

HOPE & HELPS

Scripture I clung to on the hardest days/nights:
Lamentations 3:22–24; Psalm 16:11; Acts 5:41

Helpful things people did to minister to me:
- Thirteen different men preached for me during my chemo. Each man brought gifts from their congregation, cards, prayers, and paper plates (so my wife didn't have to do dishes).
- People did my yard work and our laundry since my wife (who was nursing our new baby at the time) could not touch my chemo bedding.
- Financial gifts.
- Played with our kids.
- One church gave us $12,000, which allowed us to finish chemo debt-free!

What you should NOT say to someone in a similar circumstance:
- Don't say, "What are your chances?" to a friend in front of his wife and kids. Rather, just listen and comfort him.
- Don't pray, "Lord, may You heal him if it be your will. But if you don't …" Rather, pray to the healer to heal!
- Don't try to relate by sharing a story of a friend who had cancer. Especially if they died. Rather, simply say, "I do not understand, but I praise that we have a God who does."
- Share verses that refresh life, not condemn it.
- Don't try to fix it or solve it for him, share your thoughts on his treatment plan, or give him books on how orange juice can rid him of the tumors. Rather speak to him about something other than cancer, and sit in the ashes with him.

Hymns or songs that comforted me:
- *I Will Follow You*, Vertical Church
- *Though You Slay Me*, Shane and Shane

The hope Jesus has given me through my cancer and loss of my daughter, Hope:
Jesus meets us where we are and He hears us when we cry out to Him. In our weakness, He is our strength. Every trial we face has an eternal purpose and our loving God is using all things for our good and His glory.

ALL YOUR ANXIETY

Is there a heart o'er-bound by sor-row? Is there a
No oth-er friend so swift to help you; No oth-er
Come then at once; de - lay no long-er! Heed His en -

life weighed down by care? Come to the cross, each bur - den
friend so quick to hear. No oth - er place to leave your
treat - y kind and sweet. You need not fear a dis - ap-

bear - ing; All your anx - ie - e - ty leave it there.
bur - den; No oth - er one to hear your prayer.
point- ment; You shall find peace at the mer - cy seat.

All your anx - i - e - ty, all your care, Bring to the

mer - cy seat; leave it there. Ne - ver a bur - den He

can - not bear; Ne - ver a friend like Je - sus!

Words and music by Edward Henry Joy   ©MichaelKravchuk.com

I recall this to my mind,
therefore I wait.
The Lord's acts of mercy indeed do not end,
for His compassions do not fail.
They are new every morning;
great is Your faithfulness.
"The Lord is my portion," says my soul,
"therefore I wait for Him."
The Lord is good to those who await Him,
to the person who seeks Him.
It is good that he waits silently
for the salvation of the Lord …
for if He causes grief,
then He will have compassion
in proportion to His abundant mercy.
For He does not afflict willingly
or grieve the sons of mankind.

Lamentations 3:21–26, 32-33

Great Love

Emily Curtis

What love the Father has lavished upon us,
That we should be called the children of God.
He withholds His wrath & pours out compassion
Toward those He created out of mere dust and sod.
Rejoice, O His loved one, for you He holds dear,
He has secured our great rescue, exchanging love for our fear.
We no longer have cause for sorrow or dread,
He supplies all our needs & is our Living Bread.
Let us rejoice and sing praise to His name,
Let us be humble, seeking Christ to obtain.
He has given us life both precious and new,
He has opened our eyes to His glorious Truth.
Great things He has done, our Savior and King,
So as long as today is "today" we will sing.
For if we keep silent the very rocks will cry out,
The heavens will testify and the whole earth will shout!
So let us who are formed in the image of God,
Give full adoration and let us applaud
The works of His hands for mighty is He,
He upholds the great oceans & He loves you and me!

For His mercy toward us is great,
And the truth of the LORD is everlasting.
Praise the LORD!

Psalm 117:2

YOU FORMED MY INWARD PARTS

SUSANNE SHAW

In 2011, shortly after my second son was born, I started noticing some abnormalities with bleeding and, more specifically, when I would go to the bathroom. With that pregnancy I had preeclampsia*, so I assumed the issues were simply post-partum related and perhaps had something to do with the preeclampsia. When things did not clear up, I made an appointment with my midwife who in turn referred me to a GI (gastrointestinal) doctor. My first colonoscopy was two and a half months postpartum and I was 32 years old. The colonoscopy revealed some inflammation of my colon and I was diagnosed with "active colitis" and given a regimen of suppositories to use over the next few weeks and, after noticing some improvement, given instructions to taper off.

The next few years are hard to explain. I can best describe it like when you buy a house and there is a hideous light fixture that you just cannot wait to change. But once you move in, you notice it less and less, even though it is still there and just as hideous. It eventually blends into the surroundings and becomes less of an eyesore and, eventually, you become desensitized as to how ugly it really is. In short, you get used to it. The progression for me was a little like that. I had two more pregnancies that resulted in adding two more boys to our family, so I was busy and preoccupied. I was aware that the colitis was getting worse, and I was bleeding constantly, but I was not in pain and I was not debilitated—things were just abnormal and sometimes inconvenient. Nothing that I felt I could not live with, so eventually the abnormal became my normal.

At some point, I began to hear more about "gut health," holistic approaches, and special diets that promised to aid with healing digestive issues. I was reading everything that I could get my hands on and began incorporating some drastic diet changes. My husband, Aaron, agreed to let me see an integrative doctor to help guide me as I explored this option. I was hopeful that through careful diet and supplements, I would be able to heal my gut and resolve these issues. For over a year, maybe closer to two, I was careful with what I ate, I took all the right supplements, but things continued to steadily decline.

In early fall 2015, It was clear I needed to see my GI, but I also did not want to admit that what I was doing was not enough. Everything I was told and everything I had read all but convinced me that I could heal these issues holistically. I did not want to fail; I did not want to admit it was not working; I did not want to really acknowledge that I needed help.

And this is where I believe the story, His story, really begins.

On September 22, 2015, the pain started. I was debilitated. I had birthed four boys without medication or intervention, and I had still never felt pain this severe. It was my first ER visit because of a flare, my first morphine drip to ease the pain, and the first realization that God was using this disease to bend my will to relinquish my ill-perceived control. That single event changed everything. I became aware of my pride in still believing that I alone could fix myself, rather than wanting to see how the Lord has gifted the minds of some to become doctors and given others the ability to invent medicines to help my body when it couldn't help itself.

In the weeks that followed, I was still extremely sick. It is hard to explain what a flare is like, but it involves a lot of constant pain and an inability to eat or drink even the smallest substance. Anything you put in your mouth, the body immediately rejects, and, after a while, it is as if the body goes into survival mode. Often, there was what I can only describe as delirium because there would be days on end that I have no cognition of. There was always severe weight loss.

I received the official diagnosis of "severe ulcerative colitis." One night, following an after-hours phone call to the on-call doctor, who was too inconvenienced to address our concerns, my husband called one of his good friends, who is a cardiac surgeon with one of the local hospital systems, to ask if he had any recommendations on someone else we could see. At 9 pm that night, our friend personally contacted a GI doctor that he knew—a physician who was also a believer and best friends with a man at our church. This new doctor called me personally at 7 am the following morning and had me in his office by noon. In ways that we could not even comprehend at the time, the Lord provided not only who we needed right then, but who we would need for the next several years to come. To this day, my GI doctor has become such an integral part of our story. He has been a doctor, he has been a confidant, and he has seen me whenever I needed. He has never treated us like patients, but like family. He has indeed been a gift—part of the grace God gives during trials.

*high blood pressure that can occur during pregnancy and can have severe complications

Journal Entry
September 29, 2015

When you've been unwell for going on 12 days and today has been another hard one, but you leave for a brief time to gather last-minute birthday decorations for your second- born child because your husband is working one and a half hours away today and will be late On the drive home, you tell your boys that you're going to collapse when you get home, and they want to know what "collapse" is and then think it's a riot that mommy is going to "fall on the floor," but you really feel as though you might, and you open it to this: enough food to feed our army for days. Borrowed movies since the boys are probably getting tired of their own and new hot wheels for them to play with. And a love note from a friend that you've not even told you've been ill. And she tells you that meals will be brought to your door for what seems like eternity. and she'll be coming to take your boys—all your boys—Friday and overnight so you can rest.

And then you have a special and unique opportunity, through grateful tears, to affirm to your boys that, "SEE?! God knows! and He loves us and he takes care of us! SEE?!" And this, this blessing, this grace, that He uses to meet needs and uplift spirits. I am truly lost for adequate words of thankfulness.

October 12, 2015

[my mom] came 650 miles to serve us this weekend. She did my laundry, washed my dishes, scrubbed my floors, changed our sheets, played with my boys—allowed me to rest.

The last few weeks we have been so incredibly blessed to be served by ONE, unified body of believers. Friends have selflessly watched all of our boys for appointments or taken them for full days. Meals have been brought, prayers have been lifted. Rest and care has been provided. Even as life (finally!) returns to a normal, I am still being cared for and "forced" to ease back into the routine.

Trials are certainly fire for our refinement, but I affirm that the Lord also takes delight in proving His love and faithfulness through our weaknesses. in the midst of this mere earthly hardship, there has been the (bitter) sweet blessing of sanctification, a drawing closer with the guy I love and do everyday life with, a humbling of my spirit, and, again, the overwhelming privilege of being loved on by so, so many, simply because they are loved by Christ.

I truly can't think of adequate words to express my gratefulness for those who have met our needs: physically, spiritually, and, at times, mentally. We have been prayed with and prayed over; you have encouraged us, and you have helped us bear our burdens.

This. THIS is the body of Christ (1 Peter 4:8–11).

Fall 2015 marched on and life returned to a steady. I was still on a dose of steroids as well as a small regimen of other medications trying to reduce the inflammation in my colon, stop the bleeding, and allow my body to absorb some much-needed nutrients. Imagine our surprise when, just a few months later in December 2015, we found out I was pregnant again! After all my body had just been through, was still recovering from, and the medications I was taking, it just seemed crazy.

I was elated. I was feeling a little better because, interesting to note, my symptoms usually improved somewhat during pregnancy, likely because of the automatic response of the immune system to decrease activity in an effort not to reject the fetus. As a result, with my immune system not being in constant overdrive, it helped reduce my daily symptoms. All my previous pregnancies were about as textbook perfect as they could be; I never even had morning sickness! So, despite my current health condition, I really did not expect any different outcome.

At a routine OBGYN appointment for an ultrasound on January 20, 2016, I was told there was no baby. There was a sac, and everything else looked normal, but there was just no baby. I was completely blindsided. I grieved and I recognized my pride and my confidence in previous pregnancies. I was comforted by this quote by John Piper, "Occasionally, weep deeply over the life you hoped would be. Grieve the losses. Then wash your face. Trust God. And embrace the life you have."

In April 2016, I was pregnant again.

Several weeks later, I started feeling the twinges of a flare coming on. It was about five days before my son's birthday, and I was praying that I would just be able to make it past his birthday before getting too sick. The Lord was gracious, and I was able to decorate a cake and celebrate, but just after, my body unleashed like never before. I usually refer to this flare as "the beginning of the end." It was unlike anything I had ever experienced. I could not get out of bed or eat for two weeks. We had tried to manage it on our own because of the pregnancy and just kept hoping it would pass. I knew I would get put on steroids, but I wanted to avoid that because of the baby. I lost so much weight, probably close to 20 pounds that time. We finally conceded that I was fighting a losing battle and sought help from my GI doctor. I was almost immediately put on immunotherapies, in addition to steroids, chemo pills, iron, and a slew of other daily medications.

Sue – June 2, 2016

On June 2, 2016, I lost a baby for the second time. One year later, I wrote these words:

June 2, 2017

This picture was taken exactly one year ago today. It was the first time I'd been outside in over two weeks because of a severe flare … probably my worst to date. I was desperately trying to hang onto a baby that, deep in my heart, I knew would be taken from us—for the second time in five months because of this disease. It was really the beginning of the ultimate end for me, health-wise. You probably didn't know, but I struggled hard for months after this. I was just so sad. I was very much out of control of so many things. I was tired, weak, scared, and defeated.

BUT GOD.

I see this picture and the implications of then vs. now has a profound impact on me. I am strangely thankful for what now lies behind us and now I am so hopeful for the future. "But this I call to mind and therefore I have hope: the steadfast love of the Lord never ceases; His mercies never come to an end; they are new every morning, great is your faithfulness" (Lamentations 3:21–23).

For the next couple of months following that flare and miscarriage, I was in a hard place. My head knowledge of God and His sovreignty and goodness in all things was on point, but believing it in my heart was another. I wanted deliverance and I wanted peace, but I didn't really want to believe that peace could be found unless I was delivered.

Unless I had a baby in my arms. Unless the medication worked. Unless I could have a "normal" life. Until one day, the Holy Spirit very clearly convicted my heart and I had an honest conversation with myself. This is where the rubber meets the road. This is the circumstance where I either believe what I say I do, or I don't. Either I believe God is good and sovereign in all things or I don't. There is no middle ground—it just is.

He just is. And then came the second wave of understanding that none of this was a mistake or an accident. None of this was happening to me. In fact, this was exactly the way it was supposed to be! Before the foundations of the earth were ever laid, this was the plan He set for me. This was the plan! The plan ordained just for me. When that realization sunk in, I immediately felt such a flood of emotions. Relief, peace, conviction of my pride (yet again), safety, comfort. I grabbed my Bible and a piece of paper and furiously started writing out passages of Scripture with truths about God, His nature, and my position. I needed to remind myself, to see it, and I knew I would need to remember it on the hard days. To this day, that scrap of paper, those truths, remain a lifeline when I need it.

June 29, 2016

Back on prednisone for a few months until the infusions hopefully start to take over.

So where is my gratefulness in all of this? I'm grateful that the Lord continually brings me to a place where I have to relinquish my sense of control, my pride. I'm grateful for providing a GI doctor who is a believer and whom I trust with my care. Ultimately, I'm grateful that my meager trials on this earth are but for a little while. And, while not always an easy or natural response, I can choose to rejoice because of the imperishable, undefiled, unfading inheritance that is reserved for me in heaven (1 peter 1:4).

Into the fall and winter of 2016, my health still steadily and rapidly declined. I tried to hide it much of the time, so while people knew I was sick and were praying for me, most really did not know how bad it was. There is a reason they call crohn's and ulcerative colitis the "invisible diseases." I still tried to do normal things; I still smiled and said I was managing. What they didn't see was me trying to mother four little boys from the couch. Or the diapers I had to wear. Or my lab results that showed a severe deficiency in everything my body needed. Eventually, I really could not leave the house except for GI appointments. I was just too weak and my body could not be controlled. Of course I had days of discouragment, frustration, sadness, but I still held on to what I now knew to be true: that everything was just as it was supposed to be. There was a rest in my soul.

December 5, 2016

Some days are just hard. Some years are just hard. And sometimes you're just sad. You're tired. You're tired of being tired. You reach the place where you're afraid to leave the house, but you just want to be normal. So you go get a milkshake because you haven't had one in years and you want it. And really, you just want to sit in the rainy parking lot and be sad and alone and maybe a little angry. Just for a few minutes. Then you can go home and wait for tomorrow's new mercies—after you confess to your husband about the milkshake (but at least you didn't get the whipped cream).

On December 16, 2016 I dragged myself to yet another GI appointment and, through tears, begged him to take my colon out. Actually, I demanded that it be removed. I was at the end. I had no quality of life, my health was not improving, it had to go. I needed my life back. Things moved relatively quickly after that. The surgery was not only a good option, it was a necessary one. For Aaron and I, it was pretty much a no-brainer. Almost everything we had read from people who went through this procedure was a resounding "I got my life back." "It gave me my life back." And that was what we needed.

There were two surgeries. The first was about six hours long in which he removed my entire colon, my rectum, and created an ostomy. During this surgery he also created what is called a "j-pouch," where he literally created a "pouch" out of my small intestine that would eventually be attached to where my rectum was and serve to function as my colon. Once I returned home to heal for a few months, our church family became the embodiment of "bearing on anothers burdens" and becoming our hands and feet. We had meals delivered to our house almost every single day for over a month. People came and watched, or took, the boys almost every day for a month. The Lord certainly showed Aaron and I how much we needed the Body.

After three months of recovery, it was time for the second surgery. I had gotten used to the ostomy and I was just so grateful that, for the first time in so long, to be doing "normal" things. I remember crying over losing the ostomy because it was a reminder of just how much my life had been restored. A j-pouch is not always a guaranteed solution but the knowledge that I could go back to the ostomy was enough to push us forward. On May 30, 2017, I had my second surgery. This one was less complicated than the first and it wasn't long before I was well on the road of recovery. I was even back to running several miles by mid-July! It was a truly amazing, stark difference from just several months prior.

In the fall of 2017, I started feeling a little … disjointed, perhaps. I was feeling distant from God. I have described it to people as when God would do these amazing things for the Israelites and they would be so grateful and promise to worship only Him—and then eventually, they would forget. They would wander, complain, and question.

I had felt such a closeness of dependency on the Lord those last couple of years that when my life began to return to "business as usual," in a way, I felt that nearness slipping away. Like I was starting to forget how desperately I needed Him and what wonderful things He had done! I was so afraid to forget. To wander. To depend on myself again. I had heard about a ladies' Bible study that met at a local church and, while I didn't know anyone there at that time, I started to attend. After that first week, I knew I had found my place. The teaching each week breathed so much life into my soul. It was God-centered, encouraging, convicting, and left my heart filled and my mind focused on Christ and what He has done. These ladies, and their ministry, have been such a profound gift of grace.

On December 23, 2017, I had another miscarriage. It was such a different experience this time. Yes, I grieved, but I was not broken. I remember telling Aaron that, if I didn't know any better, I would have a hard time distinguishing my complete trust in God's sovereign, good plan with apathy. It was such a strange feeling to be that okay, but was also reassuring and restful. On December 30, I took apart the crib and took a picture of it in the hallway:

December 30, 2017

I am having #allthefeels about this today. Still-very-fresh sadness and heartache, but maybe even a little therapeutic? Moving forward, knowing it's all working as part of the sovereign plan for our good. I have so much peace because of that. I was asked to share at a ladies' event last Sunday and was really just speaking to myself. Do I, or don't I, believe that God is sovereign? what is my response to the hard stuff? reality check: He formed my inward parts. My body is exactly the way He intends it to be. My life is exactly the way He intended it to be.

February 11, 2018

I had a friend come up to me at church today and express how deeply sorry she was about the Christmas miscarriage and ask me how I was. Those are the friends you want around, the ones that will take a chance and bring up the hard, sad, taboo topics and ask targeted "how are you."

March 7, 2017

In my limited grasp of trials over the last couple of years, there are several puritan prayers that I have latched onto—to speak truth to myself and to change my thinking.

Guess what we found out in April 2018? Yes, I was pregnant yet again! I was certainly hopeful but dreading what I figured what coming. The weeks went on and this baby was looking and sounding healthy and everything was going smoothly. We had early DNA testing done and we finally felt confident enough to let the world know about our boy #5! People naturally assumed I wanted a girl, but the truth is that I was begging God, should He allow me this baby earth side, that it would be a boy. Those old feelings of fear and doubt were always beneath the surface, but there was also security and confidence in "the Plan," no matter the outcome. The very next day I was back in the hospital with a flare. A flare that, because of the surgeries, wasn't supposed to be happening anymore.

March 7, 2018

I was 12+ hours in the ER, morphine after morphine after morphine, almost every hour, and we couldn't get it under control. We even consented to an abdominal x-ray. I just knew this was it. The Lord was taking this baby, too. That it was just another test, another trying of my faith, to see if I did really trust His sovereign will. I spent six days without food, six days of heavy medications, of MRIs, CT scans, abdominal pain, and Max's heartbeat never faltered once. NOT ONCE. He remained steady, content, active, and unaware that there was disaster all around him. The Lord preserved Maxton Edward Shaw for His marvelous glory—that I am sure of.

The Lord has always been faithful to teach me, our family, through our trials these past years. But one year ago, He chose to teach me just as profoundly through His blessing—through His gracious favor on me and Max. To that end, Max is so much more than my rainbow baby, or wonder baby, or angel baby as his brothers have nicknamed him; he is an ever-present reminder of God's goodness to me. His faithfulness and His lovingkindness. The beauty from the ashes (Isaiah 61:1–3).

When Max was one week old, I had another flare. When hospitalized, they performed an endoscopy and pouchoscopy (basically a colonoscopy, but since I don't have a colon, it's the same procedure, just examining the pouch) and took some biopsies. I either had an infection in my pouch or Crohn's disease. My GI doctor suggested that we should do a camera endoscopy to get a full picture of my entire digestive system and small intestine. It revealed that I did indeed have Crohn's Disease. It was discouraging to know that now, this would be something I would struggle with for the rest of my life, but at the same token, it was a relief to have an answer.

This disease, this affliction, is undoubtedly a blessing in my life, in the life of my family. I truly do believe that the all-knowing, gracious Father has given me this "thorn" to keep me aware of my sin, to keep me dependant on Him, to keep me aware of His mercies and lovingkindness. I have never been more aware of my pride since all this began. I have never been more aware of my lack of self-sufficiency. I have never been more aware of what a gift health is. He promises to work all things together for our good (Romans 8:28) and I have seen the evidence of that. Not some things, ALL things. We have seen the Lord provide for us in ways we did not know we needed. We have seen the Lord work compassion in the heart of our boys, for His glory. I have seen the Lord gently reveal my sin, my weakness. We have seen the Lord prove His faithfulness and goodness. We have seen the Lord give us the beauty from the ashes.

HOPE & HELPS

Scripture I clung to on the hardest days/nights:
Psalm 23:3; Romans 8:28; Psalm 139:5, 13; Isaiah 43:1; Psalm 55:22; Philippians 4:19; Isaiah 26:3; Psalm 46:1; Revelation 21:5; 2 Corinthians 12:9; Psalm 18:2

Helpful things people did to minister to me:
Bringing food was always a huge blessing and taking my kids for a while so I could rest. I think many times it's much more helpful to either just tell someone what you are going to do, or just do it, rather than asking "let me know if there is anything I can do." Because chances are there is something you can do to help, but the person likely won't ask.

What you should NOT say to someone in a similar circumstance:
- "But at least you look good!" or "I have a friend who tried/sells/was cured. …" I know people are trying to be helpful when they offer "solutions," but you've likely already tried a myriad of things. If there was a "cure," you'd know about it. Hearing over and over what you "should try" is tiring and, eventually, really aggravating.

- Also, many people think that IBS (Irritable Bowel Syndrome) is the same as IBD (Inflammatory Bowel Disease) and they are drastically different. So often the advice they are giving you may be helpful for someone with IBS but has no relevancy to IBD.

Hymns or songs that comforted me:
- *It Is Well with My Soul*, Spafford/Bliss
- *Lord from Sorrows Deep I Call* (Psalm 42), Matt Boswell, Matt Papa
- *Dear Refuge of My Weary Soul*, Indelible Grace
- *Great Are You Lord*, All Sons & Daughters

The hope that Jesus has given me through my illness:
The assurance that all of this is working together for my good. It's all part of the plan; none of this is an accident, a surprise, or anything other than exactly how it is supposed to be. There is so much peace with believing that.

Sue with her 5 boys
2019

BE STILL MY SOUL

Katharina A. von Schlegel

Jean Sibelius

1. Be still, my soul: the Lord is on thy side. Bear patiently the
2. Be still, my soul: thy God doth undertake To guide the future,
3. Be still, my soul: when dearest friends depart, And all is darkened
4. Be still, my soul: the hour is hast-'ning on When we shall be for-
5. Be still, my soul: begin the song of praise On earth, believing,

cross of grief or pain. Leave to thy God to order and provide;
as He has the past. Thy hope, thy confidence let nothing shake;
in the vale of tears. Then shalt thou better know His love, His heart,
ever with the Lord. When disappointment, grief, and fear are gone,
to Thy Lord on high; Acknowledge Him in all thy words and ways,

In every change, He faithful will remain. Be still, my soul: thy
All now mysterious shall be bright at last. Be still, my soul: the
Who comes to soothe thy sorrow and thy fears. Be still, my soul: thy
Sorrow forgot, love's purest joys restored. Be still, my soul: when
So shall He view thee with a well-pleased eye. Be still, my soul: the

best, thy heav'n-ly Friend Through thorn-y ways leads to a joy-ful end.
waves and winds still know His voice Who ruled them while He dwelt below.
Je - sus can re - pay From His own full-ness all He takes a-way.
change and tears are past All safe and bless-ed we shall meet at last.
Sun of life di-vine Through pass-ing clouds shall but more bright-ly shine.

Katharina A. von Schlegel

©MichaelKravchuk.com

Jean Sibelius

*F*or You formed my inward parts;
You wove me in my mother's womb.
I will give thanks to You, for I am fearfully and wonderfully made;
wonderful are Your works,
and my soul knows it very well.
My frame was not hidden from You,
when I was made in secret,
and skillfully wrought in the depths of the earth;
Your eyes have seen my unformed substance;
and in Your book were all written
the days that were ordained for me,
when as yet there was not one of them.

Psalm 139:13–16

Rest

Emily Curtis

"For I know the plans I have for you," declares our holy Lord.
"Plans to bring you comfort in this dark and dreary world.
Although there will be suffering & at times your heart will fear,
Know that you are not alone, and I will draw you near.
For your eyes are dimly lit and see only pain and sorrow,
But I have created the bright morning star to rise on you tomorrow.
Persevere, My child, and do not forsake the hope that only I can bring,
For I have overcome this world and am sovereign over everything.
There is no tear that falls that your Father fails to see,
Lay down your burdens, precious one, and find your rest in Me."

Come to Me, all who are weary
and heavy-laden,
and I will give you rest.

———

Matthew 11:28

40 Minutes

Kristen Ironside

But we rejoice in our sufferings, knowing that suffering produces endurance, and endurance produces character, and character produces hope.—Romans 5:3

"Lethal." The doctor's eyes filled with tears as she uttered the word. Already, she knew the impact this diagnosis would have on me greater than I did myself. I wasn't sure if my own tears came quickly from deep sadness or slowly for lack of understanding. Regardless, a box of Kleenex was placed in my lap. The morning of January 14, 2019, had begun with excited guesses as to the gender of our second baby. I was 18 weeks along, a point where it seemed impossible to lose a baby in twenty-first century America.

My husband and I had toted our 18-month-old son along to the routine anatomy scan, only to be told minutes after the ultrasound that there were serious concerns about our baby. Later the same day, we had more scans with Maternal Fetal specialists, and then the words spilled from her mouth in that dark ultrasound room. "This is lethal to the baby. I'm so sorry."

If there has ever been a time when I was grateful for lack of understanding, lack of knowing the details I would work out in the coming months, it was then. In those first moments, there was one thing I needed to process: my baby would soon die. The problematic clue to the initial ultrasound technician was a complete absence of amniotic fluid surrounding the baby. The diagnosis causing this was confirmed later that day: unilateral renal agenesis and a unilateral multicystic dysplastic kidney. This is the medical terminology for saying that one of my baby's kidneys was absent, and the other was not functioning due to its own developmental problems. As a result of no kidney function, the baby could not produce the amniotic fluid it needed to fully develop.

The lungs take the hardest hit and become seriously underdeveloped by birth. Without functioning kidneys and lungs, a baby becomes incompatible with life outside the womb. While in the womb, the baby suffers no harm. A mother's body completely sustains its life as there is not yet a need for functioning kidneys and lungs. There was a slight risk of stillbirth, but the doctors told me that I would likely be able to carry this baby full term, and if born alive, my baby would have minutes to hours on this earth.

I prayed that the truth of scriptures I had known
for years would transform my heart and mind.

My due date was a full five months away, and the thought of walking such a long road anticipating death seemed to be one of the hardest things to fathom. My heart was torn. I wanted God to take this trial from me immediately. The weight was simply too much to bear. I also wanted God to sustain this pregnancy forever. Letting my baby go seemed impossible. But because each life is precious and created in the image of God, we chose life. We chose to pursue God rather than run from Him. We chose to wait on the Lord, and see His promises fulfilled in our lives. We chose to trust the truths we knew to be true, rather than the ever-changing emotions of difficult days. And I was terrified.

Ultrasound images are very difficult to read without amniotic fluid, so in the following weeks, I learned to grieve, but still did not know my baby's gender. My heart focused on Psalm 139:13–14. "For you formed my inward parts; you knitted me together in my mother's womb. I praise you, for I am fearfully and wonderfully made. Wonderful are your works; my soul knows it very well." We found rest in knowing that our Creator made this child just as He intended. I reminded myself incessantly of God's promises—that He was good, faithful, and loving; that He works for my good and His glory; that one day these tears would be wiped away. I prayed that the truth of scriptures I had known for years would transform my heart and mind.

In those first few days, the tears were constant. My brain couldn't process the information as quickly as it came. Yet after those days and weeks passed, the fog lifted, questions were answered, and the truths of Scripture sank deeply into my heart. Somehow people seem brave when they go through things we could never dream of doing. But if there is one thing I know, it is that that I am so far from that. This trial wasn't in my life because I'm brave enough to go through it. I haven't walked this road because I'm more courageous than the next person. I am weak, and I am frail. This did not happen to showcase my strength, but to showcase Christ's strength through my weakness. "But he said to me, 'My grace is sufficient for you, for my power is made perfect in weakness.' Therefore I will boast all the more gladly of my weaknesses, so that the power of Christ may rest upon me" (2 Corinthians 12:9). How good it is to be weak, for then we are made strong.

I was fearful of the months that lay before me—of seeing my growing belly, of the congratulatory remarks of strangers, of seeing my lifeless baby, of seeing it take its final breath. Life became a daily surrender of my fears, and the Lord soon gave my grieving heart joy in the journey. Nearly four weeks after the diagnosis, we received the results of a genetic test: our baby was a girl. The loss became much more real, and yet I determined that this sweet daughter of mine would live her life fully. I took bump photos regularly and on each passing holiday. I took snapshots at each place we went: the beach, the zoo, church, a coffee shop. I took video snippets of her big brother and daddy talking to her. I savored the subtle kicks she gave me. I saved each and every one of the hard-to-decipher ultrasound photos. I even went wedding dress shopping with her. We lived with her and we loved her as completely as we could for the time we had her. We named her Annabelle Hope, and spoke to her and about her by name.

The doctor appointments were constant. My health was regularly checked as it would be in any pregnancy, but there were also a host of additional ultrasounds to monitor Annabelle's growth and change. I was grateful for the extra times I had to see her gentle movements on the screen, but each visit seemed to end the same way: there is no change in her diagnosis. I also met with care teams from the hospital. I had a team of doctors and nurses that walked me through a long list of items to consider: specific plans should she be born still or alive, medications to make her comfortable for her short time, whether I wanted any intervention, how I could make memories and keepsakes with her while in the hospital. I even endured the difficult description of what she would look like in her final moments on earth. It was enough to tear my mama heart right open.

My care team sent me home with a list of funeral homes rather than the more traditional breastfeeding information and sleeping guidelines for pregnant women. My heart yearned to paint the ugly white walls of that extra bedroom in my house for a nursery, but instead, I spent time selecting a funeral home, securing a plot at the cemetery, and meeting with pastors about a funeral. I didn't buy packs of cute onesies to fill her drawers but selected one pretty pink dress for her to wear on her birthday. I didn't fill a box with bows in every color but selected one gorgeous white headband to match her burial dress. Each decision made my heart bleed, but the beautiful gift of time to make them was a great blessing.

At some point along the journey, I settled into what felt like a routine. It was a constant state of anticipatory grief marked by work days, bump photos, tears, joy in living with our daughter, and doctor appointments. As I slid past the 30-week mark, my heart again felt heavy. It seemed to be the final milestone, and most of Annabelle's preparations were in place. While I thought I still had two months before meeting her, it seemed too soon. I didn't realize just how soon it would be. One Sunday morning at 33 weeks, I awoke with slight discomfort. I adjusted my body uncomfortably back and forth during the sermon. I had maternity photos scheduled for later that day, and they would be the only professional photos I would have while our little family of four was all together alive. This couldn't be labor.

The contractions began to come regularly throughout the afternoon, so I prepared information for babysitters and packed a hospital bag just in case. At 6 pm, our family got those precious photos taken. We were together, alive, in one photo. The pain increased throughout the evening. By 2 am, I knew it was real labor. Babysitter, hospital bag, a little extra fast down the highway—it was happening. This beautiful and heart-wrenching journey we'd been on for 33 weeks was reaching a conclusion. Soon.

As we waited to be admitted to the hospital, my husband and I reflected on even the seemingly insignificant answers to prayer—that God allowed us to do the little things in the midst of this heartache. We got those maternity photos taken just a few hours ago. I had put together complete outfits for Annabelle to wear. We had taken pictures and videos along the journey. We had met with pastors and funeral homes about a service.

I had gotten the information to the necessary caretakers for our son. I never had to go to a doctor appointment to discover that my baby's heart had stopped beating. He gave us the strength to get through the day we heard Annabelle's diagnosis, the day we heard she was a girl, and the day we chose her spot at the cemetery. God's taken care of us for the big and the small. He would also give us the strength for the next few hours. Our final earnest prayer was that we would get to meet her alive.

By the time we were moved into a labor and delivery room, we were all surprised to see just how quickly Annabelle seemed to move. Before we knew it, the doctor told me it was time. It's time? How can a mother have the strength to deliver a baby when that is exactly what will take its life? It's like someone telling you to push your child into a busy street. It goes against all motherly instinct. Yet, it was time.

They had removed Annabelle's heartbeat monitor by this point as planned. She was breech, and we were not planning on intervention should they notice distress. The doctors' faces looked solemn. Though there was a large handful of medical personnel in the room, the silence was staggering. No machines making noise, no voices. Silence. For a minute, I sobbed. For a minute, complete weakness. For a minute, fear. Yet, it was time. I stared at the doctors' serious faces, wondering if they knew something I didn't, not daring to ask. I needed to hope. I needed to pray that my sweet girl would stay alive.

At 7:45 am, on Monday, April 29, 2019, my daughter, Annabelle Hope Ironside, was born. I finally had the courage to ask. "Is she alive?!" As the doctors placed her on my chest, I received the most wonderful answer to prayer. Yes. Annabelle, my precious daughter. She was alive. Forty minutes was all we had with our sweet Annabelle. From 7:45 to 8:25 am, Annabelle was loved unconditionally and perfectly, with every ounce of love we had in our hearts. The doctor placed her on my chest, and she cried. She cried! If you only knew how many times I had prayed I would hear her little voice.

How do you put into words what it is like to experience both the greatest sorrow and greatest thanksgiving in the same hour? How can you express the immeasurable joy of holding your crying baby against you for the first time while feeling the pain of knowing that her very life will be taken away any minute? She lay on my chest, letting out sweet but strained newborn cries. We took her in: her dark brown hair, the curve of her nose, the dimple on her chin, her deep blue eyes, her big hands, the way her face scrunched up with each cry. Our daughter. She was beautiful. I told her I loved her and spoke her sweet name endlessly.

I was unaware of time, only aware of Annabelle and every movement she made. Annabelle's cries and movements began to slow all too soon. Her cries became sparse. She seemed to lay so still between each sign of life. With every movement, my heart was filled with joy that I still had my girl. We sang "Happy Birthday." We loved her. Simply, deeply, truly … loved her. I don't know the exact second that Annabelle passed into eternity. As she calmly lay on my chest, the doctor checked for her heartbeat, and was no longer able to find one. It was peaceful, simple, quiet. My husband and I embraced, our baby girl between us. Tears flowed freely. Kind and gentle words expressed to one another, now and forever bereaved parents.

If you've never been given only one day with your child, you likely have no idea just how tightly you want to hold them, how long you want to study them, and just how much you want to memorize what that baby feels like to hold. So we held her and loved her. We smiled and laughed. Our nearly two-year-old son was soon brought to our room, and for a moment, we were like most other rooms with newborns–Daddy holding the new big brother up to see this sweet baby that for months was simply in Mommy's tummy. We took pictures, so many pictures. All 4 lbs., 13 oz. of her were weighed and measured. Annabelle's four grandparents, who all live on the other side of the country, arrived to meet her.

The next morning, my husband and I held our little girl for just a little longer. We told her we loved her and that she was beautiful a hundred more times. And though I had only just held Annabelle for the first time the day before, it was now time to set my baby girl down for the last time. I placed Annabelle in the bassinet, never to hold her in my arms again. And with a final "I love you, Annabelle," we left the hospital room without our newborn baby.

Those first few mornings, I awoke early, in tears, and read words of comfort in the Psalms. The battle between thanksgiving and sorrow raged within me. Such deep sorrow of those precious 40 minutes with Annabelle having passed so quickly and never being able to hold her again. Yet such an uprising of thanksgiving welled within my heart. Thanksgiving because I had those 33 weeks and 40 minutes along with a multitude of answered prayers along the way, and how can I possibly be angry over such an incredible gift? Joy and sorrow so intricately intertwined, a seemingly impossible coexistence, but yet it's there. There now and until the day that sorrow is supernaturally taken away, leaving only joy for eternity.

We had a beautiful celebration of Annabelle's life five days after she was born. Knowing I would never stand in line receiving countless hugs at her birthday party or wedding, I truly enjoyed her celebration. It was so special to have a host of people show up to see Annabelle in person and be reminded of the hope we have in Christ. I saw her physical body for the last time, gave her one last kiss on the forehead, and had to leave her casket behind me at the cemetery.

Soon the activity of those first days stopped. The silence returned. I wandered into my living room filled with flowers, stunning reminders of so many people that took part in making Annabelle's celebration exquisite. The floral scent was striking, and I saw pink flowers in every corner. How I would trade in the scent of flowers for the scent of a newborn, and trade in the carefully placed arrangements for hastily strewn burp rags. But this is my story. A story of love and love lost. The times of weeping and mourning became messily tangled with the times of laughing and smiling, and I learned that grief is not necessarily linear. When I found myself smiling, I wondered why I wasn't weeping, yet when I wept, I longed again for the peace that surpasses all understanding. A peace that almost seemed to weasel its way into my heart, whether my human heart wanted to accept such a gracious gift or not. And each morning, new mercies were flung on my doorstep, whether I chose to acknowledge their existence or not. The peace exists, and the mercies are persistent. Persistent because God knows no other way than to be who He is: to be faithful, good, and loving in the midst of deep hurt; to be the God of all comfort when I could sink to despair; to keep His Spirit active in my heart, giving me strength when I am at my weakest.

The vital role of the body of Christ became more real to me than ever. Since Annabelle's diagnosis, I had received a steady stream of encouraging messages and cards that continued for months after her birth. Meals had appeared regularly at my doorstep, with a full explosion of food filling our refrigerator surrounding her death. Books, mementos, flowers, gift cards, and financial contributions poured in. We deeply felt the prayers offered on our behalf from fellow believers around the globe. The kindness of others left us humbled and in awe of God's provisions in the storm.

In the months surrounding Annabelle's diagnosis and death, I never felt the need to question God with "Why me?" I felt at peace knowing that I was just like every other person on this planet, a sinner in need of a Savior. I knew I didn't deserve this suffering any more or less than the next person, so I simply told myself, "Why not me?" I felt the very real comfort of God and support of the church body giving me peace month after month, and knew that God was working for my good and His glory.

It came several months after Annabelle's death. I finally broke down through tears, "God, why? Why me?" I had avoided the questions all year long, and finally, as the cards and meals stopped coming, and it seemed that everyone else moved on with healthy babies, I finally asked. "Why me? Why did my baby have to die?" I knew I would never fully know the answer. I knew my finite brain could never wrap itself around the mind of an infinite God. Yet as I mulled over what seemed to be a rhetorical question, my heart settled on the same question in a different light. I didn't like asking the question. I felt selfish for asking why. So I began to wonder from a different angle, "Why me? Why would the holy God of the universe save someone such as I? Why would my God go through His own pain of child loss to rescue a despicable sinner like me?" That is the truth I would never understand. "For my thoughts are not your thoughts, neither are your ways my ways, declares the Lord. For as the heavens are higher than the earth, so are my ways higher than your ways and my thoughts than your thoughts" (Isaiah 55:8).

If I can find rest never fully understanding why a merciful God would lavish on me the eternal gift of salvation, shall I not also trust the same God in my temporal pain? If the eternal security of both Annabelle and me is placed in His hands, shall I question His perfect timing in her number of days? How could I dare shake my finger at God when He has broken His body for mine? I have seen God provide for me in miraculous ways as time passes, and each day He has renewed my strength, allowing me to move forward, stay active, get back to work, and care for my family again.

But I realize my journey with Annabelle is not a finished chapter in my life. I didn't make it through her first Christmas and first birthday only to close her memory box and slap a naive grin on my face as I continue through life. Annabelle's life is an open-ended chapter, and it seems I'll never quite know how it will end. The grief over her death, the joy in her life, and the hope that she has pointed me toward are a part of every day. The grief stirs compassion in my heart, the joy lets me shout about God's provisions from the mountaintops, and the hope draws me toward Christ. Life has become a daily surrender of my plans for His, an often-renewed prayer of "Not my will, but Yours," and an expression of the most genuine joy I have been given in the midst of heartache.

And so I find myself rejoicing in my suffering. I pray that my suffering continues to sanctify me toward more endurance and character, and I most certainly see that my suffering has produced hope. Hope: a strong and confident expectation. It is a fitting middle name for my girl as I reflect on the hope that I have, our strong and confident expectation that Christ will fulfill His promises and that we can find strength in His faithfulness. Hope, not in the doctors or in my precious baby's life, but in Christ and our future with Him. I have hope in the fact that He paid my penalty for my sin and will welcome me into His kingdom for all eternity. I have hope of seeing my own Annabelle Hope again in perfect peace. And for the rest of my life here on earth, I not only have hope of what is to come for eternity, but for a peace that surpasses all understanding even in my lifetime. I have hope in the promises of God, that this is for His glory and my good, and that I will be able to encourage others who go through similar suffering. Hope that God plans to prosper me and not harm me. So. Much. Hope.

I have hope in the promises of God,
that this is for His glory and my good,
and that I will be able to encourage others
who go through similar suffering.

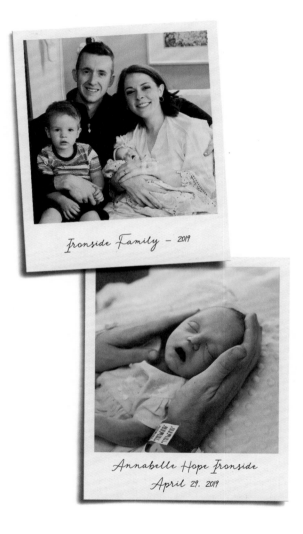

Ironside Family – 2019

Annabelle Hope Ironside
April 29, 2019

HOPE & HELPS

Scripture I clung to on the hardest days/nights:
Psalm 139; Psalm 145; Romans 8; Joshua 1:9; Romans 5:3; Philippians 4:7; Jeremiah 29:11; Revelation 21:4; Matthew 26:39; 2 Corinthians 4:16–18; Ecclesiastes 3:1–4

Helpful things people did to minister to me:
- People brought meals both before and after Annabelle's birth.
- Gift cards and financial contributions.
- Fellowship through walks/coffee dates/lunch.
- Gifts of books to help with devotions or grief.
- Gifts of unique mementos to remember Annabelle.
- Encouraging texts and cards (especially on difficult appointment days).
- People made phone calls for us (to funeral homes/cemeteries).
- Simply asking about how we were doing or about Annabelle herself.

What you should NOT say to someone in a similar circumstance:
- Saying nothing at all.
- Phrases that downplay the situation or simply try to cheer up the person. "You're young." "At least you already have a son." "It could be worse."
- Phrases that aren't true or provide false hope. "It'll be ok." "God will work a miracle." "Don't worry, I'm sure you'll have another kid."
- "Let me know if you need anything." This puts the burden back on the one suffering.

Hymns or songs that comforted me:
- *It Is Well with My Soul*, Spafford/Bliss
- *Blessings*, Laura Story
- *Yet Not I But Through Christ in Me*, CityAlight

The hope Jesus has given me through my loss of Annabelle:
The loss of Annabelle has given me hope in the eternal rather than the temporal and the unseen rather than the seen. It has taught me that the worth of my own plans for my life pale in comparison to the plans the Lord has for me. As precious as each family member and friend in our lives can be, our hope in both this life and the next cannot be dependent on them, but only our Savior. Turning over those temporal gifts to God allows us to rejoice in the hope of one day living with no tears and no pain altogether.

IT IS WELL WITH MY SOUL

Horatio G. Spafford   ©MichaelKravchuk.com   Philip P. Bliss

Therefore we do not lose heart,
but though our outer man is decaying,
yet our inner man is being renewed day by day.
For momentary, light affliction is producing
for us an eternal weight of glory far beyond
all comparison, while we look not at the things
which are seen, but at the things which are
not seen; for the things which are seen are temporal,
but the things which are not seen are eternal.

2 Corinthians 4:16–18

Peace

Emily Curtis

Father God in Heaven, the one who sees all things,
Look down upon my sorrow and hide me in Your wings.
Give me peace while storms surround me and let me not be shaken.
Plant deep within my soul the truth that I am not forsaken.
Grant to me Your mercy while I still do mourn,
And in time replace with roses where I now see only thorns.
Take this bitter cup and the tears of all my sorrow,
Lead me by streams of water where hope is shining for tomorrow.

He will cover you with His pinions,
and under His wings you may seek refuge;
His faithfulness is a shield and bulwark.

Psalm 91:4

JOURNEY OF GRACE

JEAN (SEWARD) MCCOLLUM

For my thoughts are not your thoughts, neither are your ways my ways, declares the Lord. For as the heavens are higher than the earth, so are my ways higher than your ways, and my thoughts than your thoughts.—Isaiah 58:8–9

Married 27 years, Pete and I had four active children, ages 12 to 20—two at home and two in college. We enjoyed relationships at our church and served together in the children's ministry where Pete was beloved by all waist-high or below. His uninhibited personality drew kids to him. Adults also found him engaging as he loved to talk about the deep things of God as well as the latest college football score. We enjoyed hosting friends and young people at our home. Pete had made our yard a delightful playground with ziplines, treehouses, tunnels, and he was the king of flashlight tag. His relational skills also aided his small used car business where he navigated employee and customer challenges daily. We had hopes and dreams for our future together despite struggling through many rough edges in our marriage. As we envisioned the years ahead, our desire was to grow in our love for Christ and for each other. We could never have imagined how this desire would be realized.

After a persistent cold that lasted most of January, Pete decided to see our family doctor. This visit began with a chest x-ray which then led to one test after another. The test results from his lingering cold changed our lives forever. As we waited for doctors to explain their findings, we reminded each other that the Lord was in control of all things, and that He was good. He had sustained us through the unexpected death of our 18-month-old daughter many years before, and He would be with us now. A biopsy revealed that he had melanoma on his liver and his lung: Stage IV cancer. The moments we had once taken for granted suddenly were precious. Even though the doctor who initially removed the melanoma from Pete's back told him that if the melanoma ever went to his vital organs, it would be a death sentence; Pete's new doctor thought otherwise. Nevertheless, Pete felt fine physically once the cold passed and believed that he would beat this a second time as well.

We followed all the medical advice we were given, but our ultimate trust rested in the hands of the Trustworthy One. Psalm 62:5–8 became the cry of our hearts. "Yes, my soul, find rest in God; my hope comes from Him. Truly He is my rock and my salvation; He is my fortress; I will not be shaken. My salvation and my honor depend on God; He is my mighty rock, my refuge. Trust in Him at all times, you people; pour out your hearts to Him, for God is our refuge." As Pete struggled through the physical aspects of his treatments and the unrelenting nature of cancer which did not seem to respond to them, I took on more of his tasks at home and in his business. I found strength in the early morning hours when I would read my Bible and talk to the Lord. I felt desperate at times, but it gave me a desperation for the Lord that sustained me deeply.

Pete shared with me that one year before his cancer diagnosis he had felt like a dead shell and had asked God to bring new life into him and into our marriage. He prayed that God would restore joy in his life. In God's wisdom, this prayer was answered as we walked through the challenges of each new day. Our marriage had a renewed sense of health and sweetness as the petty irritations that once divided us became an opportunity to overlook an offense (Proverbs 19:11), to look to the interests of the other (Philippians 2:4), and to love each other as Christ loved us (John 13:34). As a result, each day became a gift.

The spring and summer were filled with the outdoors, small trips to visit family at the beach and Lake Michigan and encouragement from friends in many different and subtle ways. We tried to be more intentional with our time as a family but struggled with how to talk about things with our children. The Psalms became a solace and a steady anchor for my soul, and I poured over them daily.

But Pete began to take a turn in the fall.

"We will not fear though the earth gives way, though the mountains slip into the heart of the sea" (Psalm 46:2). For a while it did feel like the earth was giving way. Pete seemed to be declining—he couldn't keep anything down and was extremely weak. My hope was to keep him out of the hospital and somehow make the 12-hour drive to St. Louis to visit his family for Thanksgiving. God was gracious on both accounts. Pete's doctor skipped treatment and made some medication adjustments which diminished his severe nausea. We were carried, it felt, all of the way there and back. That holiday season was filled with meaning and intentionality with our children and extended family.

Throughout this time, the true character of God was being shown to us. We were coming to see that He is bigger and wiser than us and intricately involved in all our affairs, not the God of our imaginations who does things in our time, in our way or on our terms. His ways are far higher than our ways. In our affliction He drew us near and spoke quietly to our hearts through His written word. He was not a far-off force, but an intimate Father who tended to the needs of His children. He taught us to bow to His will and to be at peace trusting Him. I vividly remember asking Pete for wisdom about what I should do with potential issues around his business and regarding our children. It all felt overwhelming. "You get to go to heaven," I mused. "How am I supposed to take care of all this here by myself?" With gravity and wisdom, Pete took a deep breath and stated the words I have repeated many times over, especially regarding our children. "Jean, we're going to have to trust God with them. You're going to have to trust Him."

I kept turning to the Psalms as they gave voice to my cries and pointed me to the all-wise, all-powerful, in-control God that I clung to. "Be merciful to me, O God, be merciful to me, for in You my soul takes refuge; in the shadow of Your wings, I will take refuge, till the storms of destruction pass by. I cry out to God Most High, to God who fulfills His purpose for me" (Psalm 57:1–2).

I became a widow on February 23, one year after Pete's diagnosis. This was not my plan. But the Lord showed me His kindness as He showered me with grace that sustained me through the hard months to come. As I experienced tangible evidence of care, He showed me daily that He does indeed care for the orphan and the widow. As I desperately sought to see His hand, my eyes were able to see His workings on my behalf. "As the eyes of a maidservant look to the hand of her mistress, so our eyes look to the Lord our God, until He has mercy upon us" (Psalm 123:2).

In His grace, God helped me keep Pete's business going until I could sell it, walked me through an opportunistic lawsuit that was eventually dropped but which forced me to place the business in bankruptcy. In His perfect timing He provided a kind buyer who helped me complete things in a way that honored what Pete had begun.

Several years have passed since Pete's physical death, and God's faithfulness continues. My Bible is marbled with specific dates, each highlighting a scripture that was a light to me in the dark months after Pete's passing. I love these reminders as I continue to seek Him in the early morning hours.

Like most parents, I pray for my children, desiring each one to know and trust the Lord through all He brings them. I return often to the scriptures to remind me to trust the Lord for them as I remember some of Pete's last words to me: "Jean, we simply have to trust God. We have to trust God for our kids (he prayed for them every night by name). I have to trust God that you and they will be OK, that God will take care of you. And you need to trust God too."

I am learning to do this. And I am reminded that when the rain fell and the floods came, the Lord was my Rock. He will sustain me through all that He has chosen for me as I continue this Journey of Grace. "Everyone then who hears these words of mine and does them will be like a wise man who built his house on the rock. The rain fell, and the floods came, and the winds blew and beat on that house, but it did not fall, because it had been founded on the rock" (Matthew 7:24–25).

Pete Seward and family

Peter Newcomb Seward
June 21, 1958 — February 23, 2017

This is the work that the Lord is doing in us.
He is helping us to know, really know,
the character of God.

HOPE & HELPS

Scripture I clung to on the hardest days/nights:
The Psalms spoke to me richly; they gave words to my prayers and cries and reminded me of my loving, sovereign King who knew what He was doing and welcomed my grief and confusion.

Helpful things people did to minister to me:
- Those who showed up ministered to me the most. I appreciated texts and cards but was most blessed by having someone's physical presence.
- People who did things without asking or asked about specific needs and then helped me take care of them.
- It mattered to me to see faces at the memorial service—that people took time to come.
- Cards with a story or detail about Pete. These I've kept and treasured. Cards to my children telling of something about their dad. I had adult friends who knew how to minister well, my children's friends were less experienced, and so anyone who showed understanding to them was a blessing to me.

What you should NOT say to someone in a similar circumstance:
- "Let me know if you need anything." I couldn't muster the strength to call them, and I did not really know how sincere the offer was.
- "God will use this to help you comfort others in similar circumstances someday." A true statement but I was not ready to walk into that future reality yet. Today was enough to handle.

Hymns or songs that comforted me:
So very many! The Lord seemed to provide a song or hymn that I clung to, playing it over and over. The Psalms set to music were especially rich for me and I listened to Shane & Shane's albums on the Psalms often and sang them out loud when no one was home. "Though You Slay Me" was a battle cry I sang loudly to God.

The hope Jesus has given me through my loss of Pete:
I know that His grace will be sufficient for any difficulty that I will walk through in the future. I need not fear what may come. My worst fears will not take place—the Lord has trials for me that I will not get to imagine or choose, but His grace will be there when they come.

ALL WHO SEEK A COMFORT SURE

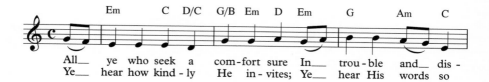

All__ ye who seek a com-fort sure In__ trou-ble and__ dis -
Ye__ hear how kind - ly He in - vites; Ye__ hear His words so

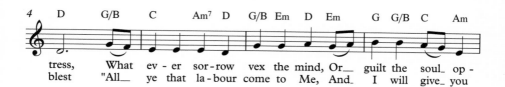

tress, What ev - er sor-row vex the mind, Or__ guilt the soul__ op -
blest "All__ ye that la-bour come to Me, And__ I will give__ you

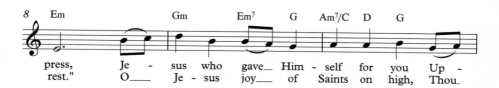

press, Je - sus who gave__ Him - self for you Up -
rest." O__ Je - sus joy__ of Saints on high, Thou__

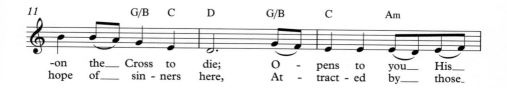

-on the__ Cross to die; O - pens to you__ His
hope of__ sin - ners here, At - tract - ed by__ those__

sa - cred Heart; O____ to that Heart__ draw nigh.
lov - ing words To__ Thee I lift____ my prayer.

18th Century Latin Text

Traditional English

*B*e gracious to me, God, be gracious to me,
    for my soul takes refuge in You;
and in the shadow of Your wings I will take refuge
        until destruction passes by.
    I will cry to God Most High,
to God who accomplishes all things for me.

———

Psalm 57:1–2

Rain

Emily Curtis

It's dark and dreary and overhead the rain is flowing down.
Upon your face is frightful dread as you wonder if you'll drown.
But I am reaching down to you and will take you by the hand
I am the master of the storms and I will help you stand.
Fear not, for I am with you, you need not be dismayed.
I am your shelter from the thundering storm and I bend down when you pray.
Your sorrow's not unnoticed, nor is your fear unseen.
Lay down your heavy burden and rest your soul in Me.
Let my feathers be your refuge, and know my promises will keep.
I will sustain you in the darkness and I will uphold you in the deep.
So when your soul is weary from the raging sea
And when there's only pouring rain for as far as you can see
My child, do not lose faith and panic that you'll drown
For I will raise you up and set your foot on solid ground.

Because He has inclined His ear to me,
therefore I will call upon Him as long as I live.

Psalm 116:2

A Tiny Miracle

Jill Aguiar

"Holy, Holy, Holy, Lord God Almighty, all Thy works shall praise Thy name in earth and sky and sea!" As we sang this song of praise to God, and the words rang out through the cathedral at the end of our wedding ceremony on a warm July day in 2010, questions coursed through my mind. "What will we face in the future? What joys will we behold? What trials will we walk through?" On this happiest of days while I stood with the man I loved and we committed our lives to each other before God and man, these were the thoughts that I wondered.

I was not fearful, but we were keenly aware of the responsibility we were assuming as we entered into the sacred union of marriage, and our supreme desire was to glorify God. However, we knew this would not come without a cost; and while we were not seeking hardship, we knew it was likely unavoidable in our future. God often works our greatest growth and glorifies Himself through trials, and my family had already been walking through a valley for several years after the sudden death of my dad. As a young teenager, I had learned about the brevity of life and had watched my mom live out the absolutes of God's promises that my dad had repeated to us again and again throughout my childhood, "God is sovereign and His way is best; God loves us and God never makes a mistake."

This firm belief in God and His truth had already carried us through deep loss and heartache, and I had no doubt that He would continue to be faithful as Tom and I began our lives together. Even still, we could not have imagined the road ahead of us, and within the next 15 months, the course of our lives would dramatically alter as we entered a trial that would become a defining point in our marriage and change our hopes and dreams from that point forward.

Father's Day weekend 2011 was one I will always remember. After several months of waiting and experiencing a miscarriage the previous month, we continued to be hopeful that each new month would bring news that we were expecting our own little baby. We both woke early on that Saturday morning, and Tom left to get in a quick bike ride before we enjoyed the rest of our day together. I had waited all week for this day to try an early pregnancy test and see if our hopes were realized. The lines on the test were clear and strong, and I quickly set up a fun surprise for Tom to see when he returned that would let him know that he was going to be a new daddy.

Through the subsequent weeks, we shared our special news with family and close friends and began to think about all the things we needed to prepare as we looked ahead to parenthood. Both Tom and I loved children and had worked with them in various capacities for many years. Having a child of our own seemed like the beginning of our own wonderful family story—something so normal and yet unique and special at the same time.

Typical pregnancy symptoms ensued, and while it was not enjoyable to be constantly ill, I was encouraged that everything seemed to be going well. We were thrilled to hear a strong heartbeat at our first doctor appointment, and we eagerly anticipated each milestone that we reached. As we entered the second trimester, I was surprised to feel worse and not better as many do once they leave those first twelve weeks behind. Still, I remembered the saying that my dad had always told his pregnant patients, "The sicker you feel, the better I feel." Being sick in pregnancy often meant things were developing as they should, so we took encouragement in this and just hoped for some relief as the days passed.

We moved apartments, found a baby crib, began to collect small baby items, and even chose a name for a boy and one for a girl so that we were fully ready to acknowledge our little one by name at our eighteen-and-a-half-week ultrasound. The day we had anticipated for so long finally materialized, and we were thrilled to hear, "It's a girl," announced by the technician shortly after beginning the procedure. We were so wrapped up in this news that we did not notice how quiet she became or that the ultrasound was so quickly over. We were shown again to the waiting room and asked to wait for the doctor; since this was our first experience, we did not think anything of it and simply enjoyed looking at the few pictures we had been given and talked about our precious little girl, Noelle Christine. We texted the exciting news to our families, and our faces were still beaming as we were brought to see the doctor, only to have our smiles replaced by questions and tears as she told us, "Your baby is not forming correctly."

We sat in stunned silence as she began to list many things that they had seen wrong in the short time that the technician had scanned, and our minds raced to keep up and understand what she was saying as we listened through the foggy grief that was already settling into our hearts. Our precious girl was far too small for her gestation, which explained why I still was not showing at nearly halfway through our pregnancy. They could not find all the chambers of her heart, her brain appeared to have fluid, the placenta was far too small and not formed correctly, and the list went on. We began to ask questions, but the doctor herself had more questions than answers since none of the signs were indicative of anything specific.

After the initial shock, I had been prepared to hear a diagnosis such as Down syndrome or even a congenital heart disorder, but nothing was clear. Instead, we were referred to a specialist who could perform a much higher-level ultrasound, but the doctor was very clear that she did not expect much hope for our little girl. She stopped short of giving us any specific actions that might happen, but we left understanding that the situation was not good.

We left that day in a cloud of grief with more questions than answers and with no idea what to expect or even what kind of expectations to have. As we cried and talked together, we recognized that God had answered our prayer, even through this "tragedy." Before becoming pregnant, we had specifically prayed for children and asked that God would only allow it in His will, His way. He had answered, not in the way we had hoped for, but it was His way, and we trusted that His way was best, even as our feelings often tried to take over and tell us differently.

The days that followed were filled with waiting, although God graciously allowed them to be busy. We had already been on standby to watch a friend's toddler as she delivered her second child, and grief mixed with joy as I held her precious little one and wondered if I would ever hold my own sweet girl. It was more than a week before we could be scheduled with the high-risk specialist, and each day seemed to take longer than the previous one. I didn't know it at the time, but God was already preparing us for many long seasons of simply waiting on Him.

So often, I just want to know an answer or "what I am facing" so that I can mentally and physically prepare for or against it. Being informed on something gives us a feeling of control, even power at times, as if knowledge can somehow change the course of events. But this was not the case. We were not God, and we had no control over the life of our tiny daughter. We could not will her existence in any way, and we simply had to trust His Word and believe that Psalm 139 was true—it was He who formed her in the secret parts of the womb, and it was He alone who would sustain her life here or choose to take her home to be with Him. This Psalm was my comfort, my joy—my solace for my tears in the days, weeks, and months to come.

The afternoon for which we had waited so long finally arrived, and the mixture of nerves I felt along with pregnancy sickness made the hours leading up to the ultrasound especially long. Tears had been very near the surface all week, and as we waited in the hospital and filled out paperwork, I again broke down as we learned that we would meet with a genetic counselor after the procedure. We had not been informed of this previously, and at the time I did not understand what role a genetic counselor would play in a journey such as ours where they thought so many things were wrong with our baby. Knowing how often people were advised to abort perfectly healthy Down syndrome babies, we were concerned that we would be advised to take this course of action after receiving the results of the test. In big, unmistakable letters, I wrote at the top of our paperwork, "PLEASE DO NOT DISCUSS ABORTION WITH US." I even found a highlighter in my purse and colored over the large letters to make sure that not one person missed that message. I knew my heart could not handle someone telling us to kill our baby, no matter what the outcome we would learn at the end of the day.

We proceeded with the technician a short time later, and she took her time, pointing out things along the way that were very "normal" when looking at your baby. Her manner was serious but kind, and we were allowed to watch the scan on a screen in front of us and took such joy in seeing our tiny girl move around without a care in the world. For the moment, she was alive and still growing, and we were thankful to have a glimpse into her little world where she was oblivious to the fact that anything was wrong. Our view of her was over far too soon, and the specialist came in almost immediately to review the results. She had been watching on a screen in another room, so she did not need to be brought up to speed. Instead, she was able to directly talk with us, sharing that she thought our baby had a chromosomal disorder called Triploidy, meaning she had an extra set of chromosomes from one parent. This can happen for a couple of reasons, but the end result is lethal to the baby.

"Incompatible with life" is how it is referred to, and the genetic counselor explained in more detail what this meant after we met with the specialist. God was gracious to give us a very understanding and kind counselor who shared that it was simply her role to help us understand the diagnosis and then walk through the process up until birth. She was there to help inform us, support us, and provide any advocating or mediating that needed to occur between ourselves and the medical team in the coming days.

We again left grief-stricken because any hope that we had had in the previous week had been dashed as they saw more clear pictures of the list of "issues" that were wrong. The specialist had informed us that some babies with Triploidy made it to birth and lived for a short time, but the most likely scenario was that one day soon, they would not find a heartbeat at a future appointment, and then they would induce delivery. Instead of the documentation to prepare for delivery, we were given contacts for "end of life" care and funeral homes. As the days passed, we settled in for the "long haul," and began to process all that we had been told. I had weekly doctor appointments, alternating between my own physician who followed my health and the specialist who followed Noelle's progress.

I researched Triploidy and found a blog of one Christian family who had experienced the same diagnosis with their little girl and had documented it through the entire process. Tears spilled often as I prepared for what we had been told and read about the timeline they anticipated. At the same time, I thanked God for the example of a couple who had chosen life and had now given us some idea of what to expect in the days and weeks to come. Their pregnancy had ended at 26 weeks, and this number unconsciously settled into my mind, even as I knew things could change for us at any moment before then.

As we proceeded with appointments and meetings and gained more information through the next month, we learned that if Noelle was born living and did not have a confirmed diagnosis of Triploidy, then they would be required to perform life-saving measures and not allow her to peacefully pass in our arms. The thought of subjecting her to unnecessary pain when the inevitable could not be avoided was horrific to us, so we proceeded with having an amniocentesis performed in order to confirm the diagnosis and ensure her comfort should she be born living.

However, to the shock of the entire medical team and then to ourselves, the test came back completely normal! Noelle's chromosomes were perfect, and they had no genetic explanation for the physical abnormalities they were seeing. A glimmer of hope entered our hearts as we realized again that nothing was certain and only God knew the plan for our little one. Still, the doctors were convinced the outcome would not change since the issues we were facing were still seemingly insurmountable. Just one of the issues, the SAC (Single Artery Cord; a normal umbilical cord should have two arteries, but an SAC has only one) was often fatal to babies just by itself; and as we approached the 26-week mark, I braced myself even more for the lack of movement and the inability to find the heartbeat at each appointment.

Throughout the weeks the days were full. The time of waiting seemed to be so long and yet simultaneously far too short at the same time. We never gave up hope and yet prepared for what we were told was to come. Joy mixed with grief as we made memories with our precious girl. We read to her, sang to her, had maternity pictures made, all while planning a funeral and making necessary plans and arrangements for a variety of scenarios.

And we waited.

Thanksgiving came, and with it, the first offer of hope from our specialists. They admitted they had never expected us to make it to this point, and they let us know that if Noelle could get to the size of 500 grams, then they would be able to fit a breathing tube down her throat when she was born. This was still no small task since she currently weighed only 300 grams, and time was not on our side. The blood flow in the cord was no longer flowing continuously to her and was instead only pulsing to her with my heartbeat. We knew this was the first step to the end of the pregnancy. In the next step, the blood flow would reverse entirely from her, resulting in her passing away in the womb.

Again, we waited and continued to plan for whatever we may face in the coming days. As we headed into December, our specialists asked us to consider admission to the hospital antepartum unit where I would be monitored until our baby was born. But in the wee hours of the morning on December 8, 2011 (the day we were meeting with our medical team to make a final decision on when to enter the hospital), the Lord made His own plans known to us. This was the day.

Enough signs had happened to notify us of some concerning changes, and after some phone calls, we were urged to make our way to the hospital, and I knew that I would not be leaving the hospital with a baby in my womb. Either I would be kept on the antepartum unit until she was born, or we would be meeting our baby this very day. We hoped for more time since we were keenly aware that our tiny baby had not reached 500 grams, and the likelihood that a breathing tube would fit down her airway was slim. A quick, initial ultrasound in the triage area allowed us to see that our precious girl was still living and moving, and the passing morning hours became a blur as we talked with doctors, specialists, and neonatologists while they tried to ascertain exactly what was happening and how to respond.

I received an injection of medication to help Noelle's underdeveloped lungs, and the hope was that I could make it another 24 hours to receive another dose. An IV was started and I was sent for another high level ultrasound—something now so familiar to us after months of specialist appointments. By late morning, I was finally settled into the room that I was told was my home until we met our baby. Monitors were hooked up, and I had just been informed that I was not to get out of bed for any reason when the door burst open and people appeared to be coming out of the walls as the room swarmed with medical personnel. The specialist informed us that the ultrasound that had just been completed revealed that the blood flow in the cord had reversed and we had moments to get Noelle out if she was to have any chance of survival.

My body was ejecting her, and the womb which had been her very imperfect, yet safe, haven had now become deadly to her. I was barraged with instructions, Tom was prepped to be in the OR, and questions were being hurled at me regarding allergies and last-minute necessities before receiving anesthesia. As I was raced down the hall to the OR, the whirlwind of activity graciously kept me from fully processing what we were facing. It was not until moments later when I had to sit completely still while they administered the anesthesia that the gravity of what was about to happen hit me with full force. Tom was not allowed to come into the OR until they had settled me, and I felt a strange sense of isolation even as people in masks swarmed around me, prepping for an emergency C-section.

Sobs rose in my throat as I gripped the arm of an unfamiliar nurse while a needle was placed in my back, and I knew that this was the end of the journey that we had now been facing for the previous 10 weeks. In a few short minutes, we would face life or death, and even if there was life, we had learned from the NICU neonatologist that the journey would be extremely difficult. The complications during our pregnancy would then be compounded with the myriad issues of extreme prematurity and the mountain of issues to overcome to just survive. As the tears flowed, my heart cried out to God for wisdom and guidance. We had made it very clear that we desired for the medical team to give our little girl a chance at life, and yet we did not want unnecessary measures taken. Our hearts could not bear the thought of her experiencing more pain if the medical procedures could not save her life. We were completely at peace that God might take our little girl to heaven, but our hearts longed to have Him make things clear and not put us in a position of deciding life or death.

We trusted that He had carried us this far and guided us every step of the way, and He would continue to do so. A calmness settled over me as I prayed, and Tom was shortly brought to my side as we waited for everything around us to take place. The room was packed with people since there was not only a team to take care of me and deliver a high-risk pregnancy, but the NICU team was also ready for whatever happened next.

We had been warned to expect a listless baby since the blood flow had reversed and she was not getting any nutrients or energy that she needed. The expectation was that if she was unresponsive or if the breathing tube would not fit down her airway, then she would be made comfortable and then given to us for us to enjoy whatever moments she had on earth. However, if she came out responsive, then they were willing to give her a fighting chance.

Moments later, to an anxiously waiting room full of people, the tiniest of sounds pierced the silence. So small, it would have been missed in any other setting, and yet it was full of emotion. Our baby girl, all 356 grams of her, was fighting mad and ready to take on the world for having been removed from her comfortable little home. Everything went into fast forward and slow motion at the same time as the NICU team went to work, and we waited with bated breath to learn whether they could successfully insert the ventilation tube. Things were not going well, and it did not appear that it was going to fit when the neonatologist finally stepped in himself and gave it a try. The Lord guided his hands exactly where they needed to go, and moments later, they held up our tiny baby for us to see before whisking her away to the NICU for much-needed treatment to help sustain her life.

For a moment, we were simply overjoyed. We were parents to a baby that had never been expected to make it this far or to be born living; and yet for the moment, she was alive, we had seen her miniature face and hands, and we had heard the sound of her little voice as she cried out. Born one day shy of 29 weeks, she still was only the size of a 20-week gestation baby, and already the reality of this was beginning to sink into our minds. Our hearts were full of thankfulness for what God had just allowed, and the hope that had been in our hearts grew even more as we considered the possibility of life, even for a few hours or days.

I could fill a book with the details of what the ensuing days held for us. The NICU is not lightly called a "rollercoaster," and we would hang between life and death for the next several weeks. Each day brought hope and gratefulness that God had allowed us more time together while at the same time bringing grief, questions, and waiting for all that she was experiencing. We continued to beg God for wisdom and clear direction, and He was always faithful to provide it just as we needed it. Weeks passed before we began to even dream of the possibility that we might take her home someday, and it would be many weeks beyond that before that dream actually became a reality.

Beyond that, through the next couple of years, the list of knowns and unknowns would continue to grow as we encountered surgeries, procedures, therapies, another near-death experience, and much more. Things were not suddenly "easy" just because life had been given. Even today, Noelle continues to face a variety of setbacks and issues in different forms; but truly, life is beautiful. Through all the ups and downs and the "hardness" of what we have encountered on a daily basis, God's faithfulness has never wavered. He has demonstrated His love and care for us over and over; and more than anything, His kindness has struck me in ways I have not before realized. Each day as I watch our precious daughter, I see His sustaining grace in our lives.

When you experience death as my family did with my dad,* you come to recognize that God will have His perfect way, and there is much peace in that, despite the horrendous pain. Walking that journey built my trust in Him, and I knew that He would continue to be the same God and carry us through whatever we experienced with Noelle. We were fully prepared for death and the possibility that we would not meet our baby until we were one day face to face in heaven. We had taken comfort in the fact that she would not experience sin on this earth and would only enjoy the perfect glory of God in heaven. But God, in His kindness, gave us a precious, undeserved gift and forever changed us from the people we were. He has continued to mold us through the last nine years as our journey has morphed into a path that is often still difficult for Noelle and yet so full of joy and hope along the way.

Yesterday, I watched our sweet girl run through the soft grass and climb trees without a care in the world, and I thanked Him once again for the simple and yet miraculous gift of a child and the privilege it is to be a mother. The overarching truths that I can still hear my dad and mom speak continue to remain: He is faithful. He is kind. He never makes a mistake. He loves His children. And He will always be sovereign and do what is best. I pray we will always love, trust, and serve Him in return.

Jill is the oldest daughter of Mark and Chris McDowell (page 203).

Noelle was born weighing 12.55 ounces — December 2011

Noelle went home weighing 3 lbs., 8 oz. — April 2012

Noelle as a happy 9 year old. — 2020

HOPE & HELPS

Scripture we clung to on the hardest days/nights:
Psalm 139

Helpful things people did to minister to us:

- Made difficult phone calls for us (such as to funeral homes).

- Made freezer meals for us; gave gift cards for food and gas (this was huge—it saved us so much time not to have to think about preparing food and gave us more time with Noelle).

- Sat with us during surgeries—this was tremendously comforting and helped us pass the time in a meaningful way.

- Provided gifts that we were able to use in the NICU for Noelle: a recorder to record ourselves praying, reading stories, singing, and talking to Noelle that could be played when I was exhausted from talking or when we were not able to be in the NICU; tiny blankets and hats, made just her size—things that could never be found in a store; and more things than I can even remember right now that are tucked away in a special wooden box that was handmade specifically for her.

What you should NOT say to someone in a similar circumstance:
- Romans 8:28. This verse is wonderful in context but quoting it to someone during a time of suffering just to "say something" or "slap on a band-aid" is not helpful.

- "God must have chosen you to walk through this because He knew you could handle it" or "God promises to never give you more than you can handle." God does not choose us for any situation because of our human ability to handle whatever comes our way. He displays His grace and power through our weakness. Scripture demonstrates this over and over again through the men and women of the Bible. Every single one of them was a flawed sinner, and we are the same—in desperate need of God's daily grace and mercy to walk faithfully with Him, especially through dark trials. It's His strength, not our own, that carries us through.

Hymns or songs that comforted us:
- *As Long As You Are Glorified*, Mark Altrogge (This song was on constant repeat and was the cry of my heart throughout the entire journey.)
- *It Is Well with My Soul*, Spafford/Bliss
- *Oh Great God*, Bob Kauflin (especially the third verse)

The hope Jesus has given us through this trial:
His kindness has shown through to us especially. Having been through the death of my dad, I had seen God's faithfulness, love, and goodness on display in unique ways. I was fully prepared to lose Noelle, knowing already from His Word and from past experience that He would prove to be faithful again and carry us through. But God chose to be kind and demonstrate His glory and faithfulness through life. He did not have to allow this, but in His sovereign grace and kindness, He blessed us with life. This blessing did not suddenly make things easy—in fact, in many ways it was more emotionally exhausting as we rode a rollercoaster between death and life for the next several months. But God. He never left us or forsook us. He carried us through the deep, dark shadows of the valley of death, time and time again, and kept our feet firmly on the Solid Rock of Hope. Our hope in Him has been strengthened. We have seen His hand at work and we know firmly that He will be true to His Word, His character, and His glory. Because of this, we can trust Him, no matter the outcome. Our Hope is secure.

O Love That Will Not Let Me Go

George Mathenson   ©MichaelKravchuk.com   Albert L. Peace

*T*o comfort all who mourn;
to grant to those who mourn in Zion—
to give them a beautiful headdress instead of ashes,
the oil of gladness instead of mourning,
the garment of praise instead of a faint spirit;
that they may be called oaks of righteousness,
the planting of the LORD, that he may be glorified.

Isaiah 61:2b-3

Courageous

Emily Curtis

The fight is fierce and everyday you're battling to win,
Surrender your fears, bow humbly your head for your courage lies within.
The very God who formed you will be your strength and guide.
He will uphold you and sustain you, remaining steady at your side.
Be strong and filled with courage, your enemy will fail.
If Christ the Lord be for you, you shall indeed prevail.
He holds the very stars in the palm of His strong hand
And He has purposely prepared each day for every man.
Again, I say "take courage," trust Him as you should
Knowing that His plans for you are altogether good.

Have I not commanded you? Be strong and courageous.
Do not be afraid; do not be discouraged,
for the Lord your God will be with you wherever you go.

Joshua 1:9

What If?
More Than Surviving
an Accident

Elizabeth Eckstrom Knussman

It seems we all have "what if's" in our lives. We second guess our decisions. I once learned that, instead of second guessing mine, I needed to trust in the sovereignty of God. I learned the hard way.

When I left high school in the upper Midwest for college, I had certain expectations. Even given some physical limitations, I had done well with balancing curricular and extracurricular life. Why should I not be able to do the same in college?

With my new portable typewriter—my graduation gift from my parents—I made my way to college, a small, faith-based liberal arts school not too far from home. I signed up for a significant course load and several extracurricular activities. My dad was working close enough to the campus that I could go home weekends with him if I chose to. Life looked all set for me.

But what I had been able to handle in high school proved to be too much for me in college. In the vernacular, I had bitten off more than I could chew. I found myself continuing to get bad grades, and because I was at a small college, the dean kept an eye on me. But I did not heed the warning signs.

Then in the second semester of my freshman year, my dad told me something I had never considered possible. The company that had employed him for more than 20 years had been purchased by another. He had been offered a transfer to their facility on the East Coast, but after he prayed and considered it, he decided to leave the company. He was going to farm full-time, and at some distance from where my college was located.

As it were, both shoes had fallen. My world was changed, and I could not handle it.

Oh, I went back to school for my sophomore year, but that was worse than my freshman year. I left school, on probation, before the academic year was over. Humbled, in tears, driven by my parents to their new farm home, I had no expectations of grace. But God provided me with pastoral and parental counsel. And physical rest I so needed.

After some weeks, I went back to look for work in the city where I had been attending college. I did not know if I would ever be allowed to re-enroll at that school. In any case, I had some growing up to do.

Later, the college graciously permitted me to return. There were, of course, limitations. I had to get my grades up, so I had to take fewer courses and make a smaller commitment to extracurricular activities than before. I was so thankful to be given a second opportunity; I was willing to do better.

I had been foolish in my impudent expectations. I had not considered that with Jesus as my sovereign Lord and Savior, I had no right to expect things to go on as before. I had so much need to grow in His grace and in the knowledge of Him and His Word. I look back with gratitude at the grace He extended to me both then and in the subsequent years. By that grace I was able to complete my college degree in 1971, a year later than I had planned. Then, I began to look for a job, but my search would be interrupted.

Because it was a Friday afternoon in early June, members of my family were not home at their farm house. My dad was in the field, and my mom and sister were in town, shopping. It would be hours before they got the phone message that changed everything. My roommates were also occupied. They would come home to a note from the police. I had finished my job search and had made plans to meet a friend for coffee. I had changed into casual clothes and taken the bus to the University of Minnesota campus in Minneapolis. From there it was a short walk to my friend, who was working in a nearby building.

God had other plans for all of us then.

I had almost reached my friend when I was sideswiped by a city bus. I was not in a car or a bus—just me on my own two feet. I have no recollection of that event. As far as I knew, one second I was waiting on the curb for the light to change and the next I was flat on my back in a hospital and a nurse was asking if I knew who the people with her were. "Well, yes, of course," I said. I wondered why she did not know. Immediately I went back to sleep. Later I learned I had a significant concussion, so I slept a lot that weekend.

My family, having heard of my accident, had to find someone to take care of their farm. Driving to where I was in hospital, they knew only that I had been involved with some sort of serious accident. Was I dead or alive? If alive, what condition was I in? How serious were my injuries? And I am sure they prayed and also asked others to pray.

That I survived the accident was amazing.

After the fact, I learned from my mom that my heart had stopped and had to be restarted. Think of those episodes on the old TV series Emergency in which the paramedics are on the site of an accident. Then think of before there were paramedics and only ambulance workers. Someone "thumped" my heart back into working order.

After nearly 50 years, aspects of that day still amaze me, including how the mirror on the side of the bus hit me in the left temple. It could have caused me to be blind in that eye. It could have been fatal. God saw to it that neither effect occurred.

I was in the hospital from Friday afternoon to Sunday afternoon; then my parents took me to their home for further recuperation. We had no idea how long it would be before I was off crutches and able to maneuver on my own again. My left foot was so swollen that for several weeks I had to wear a bread bag on it instead of a shoe. I could not even get one of my dad's shoes on. I was grateful to be able to rest, thankful that there was no employer yet, thankful that my former roommates kept me in their prayers in my absence.

I could not make it up the stairs to the bedrooms at my family home, a spacious, two-level farm home, so the family improvised. I slept in a back room that served as a den. Providentially there was a half bath that I could reach fairly easily. My long hair was matted with blood, and my mom carefully worked dry shampoo through it for days. Everyone was so patient during my recovery.

I saw both the doctor and my family pastor several times. I was attempting to understand why I survived what should have been a fatal event.

When I was home, recovering, several people pointed out Romans 8:28 to me. It did not make as much sense to me then as it does now. After about two months, relatives let me stay with them in the Twin Cities while I resumed looking for a job. I was hired by the Billy Graham Evangelistic Association—the first of several jobs I had before I met my husband.

I could go into certain "what if's" in my life prior to and subsequent to that event, but the scarier "what if's" have to do with God's character.

What if He was not what the Scriptures reveal Him to be?

Instead, I am so thankful that He is the same as when He created the heavens and the earth and all that is in them; that He is the same as when He called Abraham; as when He sent His Son incarnate to die sinless, bearing my sins, the consequences of my sins; as when He rose from the grave triumphant. I am thankful that every word written in the Bible is still "profitable for teaching, for doctrine, for reproof, for training in righteousness" (2 Timothy 3:16). I am thankful that Romans 8:28 is still true because God is. We can say what Paul said: "And we know that God causes all things to work together for good to those who love God, to those who are called according to His purpose."

There were lessons to be learned in almost 50 subsequent years, expectations that did not work out in employment situations, personal relationships, even churches. I have needed a lot of lessons in patience to humble me. No doubt I will have more remedial work in the time ahead, whatever situations God has planned for me. I need to take that long view and be grateful.

As James wrote, "Consider it all joy, my brethren, when you encounter various trials, knowing that the testing of your faith produces endurance. And let endurance have its perfect result, so that you may be perfect and complete, lacking in nothing. But if any of you lacks wisdom, let him ask of God, who gives to all generously and without reproach, and it will be given him" (James 1:2–5).

As Peter wrote, "Grace and peace be multiplied to you in the knowledge of God and of Jesus our Lord; seeing that His divine power has granted to us everything pertaining to life and godliness, through the true knowledge of Him who called us by His own glory and excellence. For by these He has granted to us His precious and magnificent promises, so that by them you may become partakers of the divine nature, having escaped the corruption that is in the world by lust. Now for this very reason also, applying all diligence, in your faith supply moral excellence, and in your moral excellence, knowledge, and in your knowledge, self-control, and in your self-control, perseverance, and in your perseverance, godliness, and in your godliness, brotherly kindness, and in your brotherly kindness, love. For if these qualities are yours, and are increasing, they render you neither useless nor unfruitful in the true knowledge of our Lord Jesus Christ. For he who lacks these qualities is blind or short-sighted, having forgotten his purification from his former sins" (2 Peter 1:2–9).

Young Elizabeth around the time of the accident

Elizabeth with her husband, Garry

I had so much need to grow in His grace and in the knowledge of Him and His Word. I look back with gratitude at the grace He extended to me both then and in the subsequent years.

HOPE & HELPS

Scripture I clung to on the hardest days/nights:
Psalm 23; Psalm 46:1–3; Psalm 145; Romans 8:26–39; Philippians 4:6–7

Helpful things people did to minister to me:
- Prayerfully sent cards with Scripture.
- Visited when I was able to have guests (but were sensitive to my strength limits).

What you should NOT say to someone in a similar circumstance:
- You will recover soon.
- Why did you get yourself into this predicament?
- Scars heal.
- You should be thankful it wasn't worse.

Hymns or songs that comforted me:
- *And Can It Be*, Charles Wesley
- *Children of the Heavenly Father*, Sandell Bergh and Olson
- *Day by Day*, Sandell Bergh
- *Like a River Glorious*, Havergal

The hope Jesus has given me through this trial:
- He will never leave nor forsake me (Hebrews 13:8).
- He is with me to the end of the age (Matthew 28:20).
- I will be with Him (1 John3:1–3).
- He always knows what He is doing even when I do not understand (Psalm 119:130).

DAY BY DAY

Carolina Sandell Bergh

Oscar Ahnfelt

*Rejoice in the Lord always;
again I will say, rejoice!
Let your gentle spirit be known to all men.
The Lord is near.
Be anxious for nothing,
but in everything by prayer and supplication
with thanksgiving
let your requests be made known to God.
And the peace of God,
which surpasses all comprehension,
will guard your hearts and your minds
in Christ Jesus.*

Philippians 4:4–6

Joy in the Mourning

Emily Curtis

"There shall by joy in the morning" I hear them say,
But when I awake I'm in continual pain.

This bitter cup, I humbly hold,
And approach the Throne, frail, yet bold.

"Father," I cry, "bend your ear,
Take this cup and draw me near."

"Remove this trial, pity my plea!"
Then through the pages of Scripture He spoke me.

"Dear one, my mercies are new each morn,
I am with you in joy and when you're forlorn."

"Although I may not remove your plight,
I will go before you and help you fight."

I opened my eyes from desperate prayer,
And found joy in the mourning,
At rest in His care.

*Come to Me, all you who labor and are heavy laden, and I will give you rest.
Take My yoke upon you and learn from Me, for I am gentle and lowly in heart,
and you will find rest for your souls. For My yoke is easy and My burden is light.*

Matthew 11:28–30

Sweet 16

Chuck Kirchner

May 18, 2018, our sixteenth anniversary. It would also be the day that my two young boys and I laid my beautiful wife to rest after a seven-year battle with metastatic breast cancer.

What a gift life is. What a blessing, despite all my flaws, to be truly loved by such a beautiful soul. "An excellent wife, who can find? For her worth is far above jewels. The heart of her husband trusts in her. And he will have no lack of gain." (Proverbs 31:10–11). My heart did trust in her and I had no lack of gain. How precious those days became when we first heard that this life would be drawing to a close for Jessica.

We first met in 1998. Alan, a guy I played rugby with, knew I worked in the science field and that Jessica was interested in working in the science field. I had been in the military prior to college so I was 3-5 years older than a lot of my contemporaries. So naturally he told her, "You should meet this really old guy I play rugby with." We did meet, hit it off, and started dating. And about a year later we started working together.

I grew up Irish Roman Catholic. I went to CCD (catechism classes teaching Catholic doctrine) once during the week and to mass on Sundays. As a teenager I remember drinking alcohol at several youth group events. Jessica had gone with a friend to a youth group where Scripture was preached to some degree but it didn't really take root. Except for an occasional mass, I did not really go to church during the military or college. After college I had started to attend mass again and when Jessica and I started dating she started to come to mass with me. She did not know when you were supposed to stand, sit, or kneel. She also didn't know that when the priest said, "Peace be to you" that you were supposed to respond with an "and also with you." She was never very comfortable there.

While we were dating, we noticed a lump almost where the collar bone meets the deltoid muscle on Jessica. We did not think much of it at first but had it checked out. It turned out to be breast cancer and she would have to undergo several surgeries, chemo, and radiation at the young age of 22. Many good stories there to tell but suffice to say that the Lord kept His wing over us through that entire time.

A girl that we both worked with had gone on a missionary trip to Haiti. She was showing us some pictures and telling about the orphanage they helped build. I was enthralled. I asked her if I could go next time she went. Jessica was interested in that as well. They had a trip planned the following year and about six months prior to going, Jessica and I started attending that church. It was there that we both heard the Scriptures preached for the first time. God started really opening our hearts to His truth.

On the mission trip, we ended up going to Mirabela, Haiti, and helped build a church there. There were 12 of us that went from our church along with 42 youth-group members from a nearby church. I remember one morning when Jessica had lots of reasons to complain: she didn't feel well, we were short of water, the food was questionable, and more. I don't think I would have thought twice if I had heard her gripe, but she didn't complain at all. As we were out there under the hot sun, several of us were carrying large stones to help build a retaining wall. There was a moment

I was just able to watch her work from a distance. She was up the hill from me and she didn't notice me watching her. She, too, was carrying rocks. She was dirty, sweaty, and beautiful. Despite all that had been against her, she wasn't complaining but rather working hard and had such a look of joy and peace on her face.

I knew she was the one for me. On our last day there we all gathered around the pool at the hotel in Port-Au-Prince. In front of everyone, I proposed to her. My pastor gave me a little Haitian wooden ring to give to Jessica until we could pick out something proper.

We had been living very worldly, but as we came to know the Lord, we stopped doing things our way and started doing things His way. His way is SO MUCH BETTER. We would go on to get married in May 2002. We worked together for several years and very much enjoyed that. We had many of the same friends and were able to have lunch together a lot.

Jessica and I had grown up in homes where Scripture was not taught. Hearing Scripture, we began to see the beautiful picture of love that God paints. I was very blessed in that, once we became Christians, we both strove for God's kind of love. It was wonderful. I remember one time, early in our marriage and Christian walk, she had gone to a party with some girls from work. At some point in the evening, the girls started going around and each had to tell a bit of dirty laundry about their husband. But Jessica would not do it even in the face of huge peer pressure. She just refused to dishonor me. When I heard that story, I felt so honored and respected. Not that there was not dirty laundry for her to share, but she would not disrespect me to others. I smile even now thinking back on that.

We were both far from perfect in many things. The Lord was very gracious to grow us equally in our Christian walks. I have seen several families where either the husband or the wife embraces the faith the way Christian did in the *Pilgrims Progress** and the other flounders as an "infant" Christian if a Christian at all. I have great sympathy for the faithful spouse in that situation. There were times where one of us might be a little ahead of the other but not much and not for long. I am eternally thankful for that.

Early in our walk with the Lord, Jessica was very uncomfortable around teenagers. She was also praying for me that I would find a way to get more plugged into the church. The Lord would answer her prayer by making me the lay youth pastor at our church. I got plugged in and she got thrust in front of teenagers. But what a time of growth for us. Having to teach the Word was amazing for me and Jessica found such a profound love for those kids. Serving others together really grew us closer together as well.

We weren't sure if we would be able to have kids after all the surgeries and chemo. One day, Jessica had a lot of stomach pain. We went to the doctor and he told us good news and bad news. The bad news was we had a miscarriage. The good news was we could get pregnant. That was a heartbreaking time. But a year or two later we would give birth to our first son, Joshua, in 2006. We would go on to have two more miscarriages, one several months into the pregnancy. Then we had our second son, Zachary, in 2009.

Being together as a young family was the greatest joy my heart has ever experienced. In January 2011, Jessica traveled by herself to see her mother in Pittsburg, Pennsylvania. While out hiking, she made a misstep. She thought she had pulled a muscle in her back. It ached for a few days until she got home. That night she woke me up and told me to take her to the hospital. While there she was diagnosed with double pneumonia. They gave her antibiotics and that cleared up the pneumonia and she was doing much better. However, the cough did not go away. After about a month it became very concerning so we went to see a pulmonologist. An MRI showed spots on her esophagus and lung. He did an endoscope and took a biopsy of one of the spots.

They called us in the next day. That is when the doctor told us the cancer had returned. Jessica, the doctor, and I all cried in the office that day. Outside were a couple of very good friends of ours and our pastor. Many more tears and prayers in the parking lot. The doctor referred us to an oncologist. The oncologist told us up front that there was no cure for this and what to expect. In time, I would be very appreciative of his honesty through the whole process.

One of the things the doctor told us early on was that if the medicine worked, we might have some time. If the medicine didn't work, it probably wouldn't be long. This type of breast cancer was aggressive. We had a three-year-old son and a baby. I came home and told my older son that mommy was very sick. His first question was "Is she going to heaven?" I was freaking out at the thought of losing her soon and having to handle a baby and a toddler through that. God provided us comfort in His Word—the saints He surrounded us with and in prayer together.

After about a month of chemo, losing hair, Jessica having to quit her job to go on disability, the moment came to do another MRI. By the Lord's good grace, the medicine was working and the side effects from the chemo, though not wonderful, were livable. We would wind up with about seven more wonderful years together.

The church came out and did all kinds of work on the house, including putting a new roof on the house. Many meals and lots of love were poured on us. And, most importantly, lots of prayers were said on our behalf. Do not ever discount the importance of your love to someone hurting, no matter how trivial it seems.

Jessica started homeschooling the boys and that was the most wonderful thing ever. Many pages I could write on the blessings of those efforts. During that time, we had an opportunity to take a long vacation. We ended up taking a five-week RV trip together. We paid $5,000 in cash for a 1988 Class C "Sanford and Son Special" RV. We figured if it blew up at least we would not be in the poorhouse and we did not have to worry about rental/lease agreements. We all (dog included) had a wonderful time in travels that took us from North Carolina to Georgia, Florida, Texas, New Mexico, and Alabama. We covered over 5,000 miles and quickly sold the RV like a grenade without the pin in it! It was a wonderful time and I kept a diary. The photo book we made of the trip is a treasured keepsake. We had hoped to do it again in 2017 but that was not to be.

Chemotherapy provided plenty of opportunities for feeling bad, which, at times, gave way to selfish or covetous reactions by Jessica. However, despite her sinful nature, our last seven years together were amazing. Everything becomes more precious when you know your time is limited. In truth, our time is always limited. Tomorrow is never promised.

Jessica, although she felt wholly unworthy of Him, loved Jesus Christ with all her heart. She also loved serving in His church. She had a great gift of service and organization. Even on days when she did not feel well, she got a lot of joy from helping out wherever she could. She was never afraid to do the dishes or some other no-credit-no-glory duty that just needed doing. She did not have any desire to be the center of attention. She just loved to serve and would jump in wherever she found a need. I remember many days where she would tell me things like "I feel terrible, I need to go home and rest. Just let me finish this." She gave of herself until she just couldn't anymore. Losing your abilities and losing your faculties can be very humiliating.

As the disease progressed, she would lose the ability to attend events such as the women's retreats at church. She would still find joy in helping send out emails or doing whatever she could despite her limitations. Eventually her eyes would hurt so bad it became impossible to read. Our pastor's wife recorded herself reading several of Jessica's favorite Psalms and several other scriptures. What a precious gift to be able to hear a sweet, familiar, loving voice reading words of comfort.

When that day comes for us—and it will come—we may, like Jessica, wonder if we are truly loved by the Father. We may wonder if we prayed enough, loved enough, served enough, read Scripture enough. The answer is no. No, we did not do enough. Ever. But salvation, praise the Lord, is not based on our efforts but on Jesus's efforts. Facing death can be very scary, even for a believer. That is OK. It is God Himself who grants us faith. It is by this gift of faith that the saints of old were saved. It is by this gift of faith that the apostles were saved and many were healed while Jesus walked this earth. It is by this gift of faith we are saved now and it will be by this gift of faith that those that are His will be saved in the future. That is where our hope rests and we all need reminding of that. Read Hebrews, chapter 11 to learn more about faith.

Apart from this God, there is NO hope. But with this God there is a hope that quiets the soul. A hope that He is there with us no matter what trials or tribulations or persecutions befall us in this life. This is not our home. Our home is with Him. We seek that kingdom. We seek that king. When we get married, we often picture growing old together. May that be you, Lord willing, but keep God first. God is the one thing that does not change in our entire lives. He was there at the beginning and He will be there at the end. In the months leading up to Jessica's death, there were times where she just couldn't stop crying. Sometimes all you can do is fix your hope on Jesus.

I do not think you ever get over losing somebody you love that deeply. It just becomes part of who you are. There is not a day that goes by that I do not think of her and miss her. It has been two years, three months and four days since she passed at the time of this writing. Every day is precious, every day is a gift from the Lord. I pray you find courage to face the day and comfort in the loving arms of our Lord and Savior Christ Jesus. Thank you for allowing me to share some of my story.

*The *Pilgrim's Progress*, written by John Bunyan in 1678, is the second-most published book, only behind the Bible. I highly recommend reading it.

Apart from this God, there is NO hope.
But with this God there is a hope that quiets the soul.
A hope that He is there with us no matter what trials or
tribulations or persecutions befall us in this life.

Chuck and Jessica with
their two boys ~ 2015

Chuck and Jessica ~ 2017

Jessica Kirchner
August 25, 1976 ~ May 09, 2013

HOPE & HELPS

Scripture we clung to on the hardest days/nights:
Hebrews 13:5; Romans 5:1–5; Philippians 1:21, 23–24

Helpful things people did to minister to us:

- Loved us.

- Brought meals before and after.

- Gift cards.

- Offering to watch the children. Many people offered to watch but were only available when childcare wasn't needed. I probably would not have thought of it before, but now I would be willing to take a sick day off work, if able, to fulfill a need for someone else. Permanent solutions may need to be found but in the meantime that is very helpful. You'll probably only get asked once.

- Call to check in. Doesn't have to be heavy. "Hey, I was just thinking about you and was calling just to say hey." Convey your love.

- The pastor that married us sent us $100 per month to help pay to clean the house for two years.

What you should NOT say to someone in a similar circumstance:

- "Oh, I know somebody that died from that."

- "God will heal her." Rather say, "I'll pray that the Lord will give you grace and strength to endure whatever this life holds and just for the record I'm not giving up hope on a miraculous healing."

Hymns or songs that comforted us:
We listened to a lot of Christian music but David Crowder was by far our favorite.

The hope Jesus has given me through my loss of Jessica:
The hope that this life is not all there is. Knowledge that it is our personal relationship with God that is first and foremost. So often when we get married we view the faith walk as God and my wife and I. Lord willing, you will spend a lifetime together and leave behind a wonderful testimony. But whatever trials, tribulations, or persecutions come in this world, God is sovereign in them all and is rightly due the praise. We must always, as a good soldier, be ready to carry on. After all, Jesus is the only one who is constant in this life. Like Christian in The Pilgrim's Progress, even if all turn away from Christ, we must do what is right and we must be ready to go it alone.

Be Thou My Vision

Dallan Forgaill
arranged by Eleanor H. Hull

Dallan Forgaill   Arranged by Eleanor H. Hull

*Therefore, having been justified by faith,
we have peace with God through our
Lord Jesus Christ, through whom also we have
obtained our introduction by faith
into this grace in which we stand;
and we exult in hope of the glory of God.
And not only this, but we also exult in our tribulations,
knowing that tribulation brings about perseverance;
and perseverance, proven character;
and proven character, hope;
and hope does not disappoint,
because the love of God has been poured out
within our hearts through the Holy Spirit
who was given to us.*

Romans 5:1–5

My Beloved

Emily Curtis

My darling beloved,
What joy you have brought throughout these many years,
You were my most treasured gift,
My truest of friends and the laughter in my tears.

You radiated beauty that came from within,
As a reflection of the love you carried for Him.
The Lord Jesus Christ was your anchor and hope,
He gave you such courage and strength to cope
With the trials He deemed good for you, Love,
And your faithfulness throughout was a grace from above.

More precious than rubies and the finest of gold,
Was your love to me and your hand to hold.
We walked hand in hand through joy and through fire,
And when things were the hardest, our praise rose still higher.
For we know the One Who Knows All Things,
And can trust Him throughout the trials He brings.

His grace is sufficient and His promises true,
And so I rejoice knowing I'll be together with you,
Where there is no sorrow, no tears and no pain,
And we will worship our Savior together again.

My radiant wife, now crowned with jewels,
Walking with Jesus beside crystal pools.
I'll love you and miss you till I see you in glory,
And I'll cry tears of joy as I tell our love story.

An excellent wife, who can find? She is far more precious than jewels.
The heart of her husband trusts in her, and he will have no lack of gain.

Proverbs 31:10-11

Clinging to Christ

Stephanie Messer

Saturday, February 18, 2017, began like so many of our Saturdays. It was a warm day, which was also not unusual for North Carolina. We loved a break from the cold weather. We got up and began to clean up the yard, put down grass seed, and get ready for spring.

Our oldest son, Samuel, was home from college for the weekend. Our youngest son, Gabe, was looking forward to playing outside with friends. We had planned to grill out and have dinner together as a family, as those opportunities became fewer with one away at college. Jason, our middle son, had his own plans—getting the truck washed and breakfast at Waffle House. He was waiting for the next text from friends to plan the rest of his day.

About midday he and his friends decided they wanted to go hiking. They planned to meet at Hanging Rock State Park at 4:30. We negotiated a compromise. He would help out around the house until then, but he would be back by 7:30 for dinner together. Plenty of time for a hike. He walked out the door about 4:00. I had my head in the freezer for dinner prep. Ben was in the garage.

That would be the last time we would see him outside of his hospital bed.

The day went on as usual until 7:30. Jason was not home for dinner. We admittedly were annoyed because our first thought was that he lost track of time. Dinner came and went. Cleanup came and went. At 8:30 we got a call from a number that we did not recognize. I answered. That was the beginning of what was the biggest trial of our lives so far.

Jason had been involved in a fall. The call was a life flight nurse. She told us that Jason had been in an accident but gave us very few details. Our reaction was fear and confusion, but it never crossed our mind that Jason might die from his injuries. She told us to meet them at the hospital. We dropped everything and raced the 30 miles to the hospital.

Beginning at that moment our faith in a sovereign God would be tested. Not only tested but held to the fire in a way that we could not have imagined. As we arrived at the hospital, details of Jason's fall and rescue began to be revealed to us. At approximately 6:30 that night, Jason had fallen 60 feet into a crevice of a mountain, requiring dozens of rescuers to reach him. In order to get him to the waiting helicopter, they had to use ropes, pulleys, and ATVs to bring him down from the mountain. It took them hours.

We learned that two of the EMTs that administered life-saving measures were faithful members of our church body—God's perfect timing and the first of many gifts of grace from our Lord. During that time, we were eating the dinner that we had planned to share together. We were still oblivious to what was going on until we received the call at 8:30.

As we waited for the helicopter to arrive at the hospital, we still had no idea of the gravity of the situation. We were ushered into a room and given very little information even as he was brought into the hospital. Our youth pastor, Danny, had arrived by this time along with other church members and my parents. The longer we were in the small room, the more it began to dawn on us how serious it was.

As the weight of the moment pressed in on us, we had a strong desire to hear Scripture read for comfort. Danny read several passages, but the one that stood out to us was Hebrews 4:13–16 and particularly verse 15. It remains with us today: "For we do not have a high priest who cannot sympathize with our weakness, but One who has been tempted in all things as we are, yet without sin."

As the evening turned into night the doctors were still giving us limited information and many who had come to support us began to filter home. Samuel took Gabe home. It was just my husband, Ben, and me. We were finally led to the Trauma ICU waiting room at about 1:00 in the morning. Jason was unconscious. His lungs were not properly inflating. Jason's brain was swelling and he had two broken arms and a broken wrist.

At about 2:00 am, the doctor finally came out to give us information. He did not have good news, in fact he plainly told us that if this last procedure did not work then Jason would die tonight. The weight of that news shook us to our core. The very same High Priest, Jesus Christ our Lord, that we had read about earlier, was the only person who could sympathize with us in that dark, lonely hour. We were in a pit of weakness and tempted to despair. We needed God's mercy.

Our hearts were breaking over our son that night. Words that we could not utter, God knew and heard and lovingly drew us to the "throne of grace" as it is said in verse 16 of Hebrews, chapter 4, "Therefore let us draw near with confidence to the throne of grace, so that we may receive with mercy and find grace to help in time of need."

In God's perfect will, Jason responded to the treatment and survived the night. We were able to see him and be near him. To say he was fragile was an understatement. As we took turns sitting by his bedside, we were still in disbelief. The Lord was using the medical expertise of doctors to sustain his life. The night turned to morning. That was Day 1. The next 24 days were a roller coaster—ups and downs, endless medical terms, and procedures. Things too hard to understand and wrap our brains around. We were working hard to understand from the doctors just what was going on with Jason.

The doctors were fighting two battles. His head trauma and his lung damage. Both were equally severe. One day we would see a decline and the next day we would see improvement. Sometimes that would happen from hour to hour. Another of God's graces would be revealed in the next day or so. We had a small problem. So many texts, emails, and phone calls were coming in, that we could not handle them. A dear friend of ours set up a Facebook page for us to update as often as we could and that would serve as a help in answering all those calls.

But this would be way more than an info page about the condition of our son. This turned into a platform for the proclamation of the gospel. Almost 2,500 people were tuned in to that page and so many more as folks shared. They were given a daily gospel message in addition to an update on Jason. We included scripture, as well as questions posed as to what the readers own fate would be when the Lord called them home. You see, we realized that this was not about Jason, or us, or anyone else. It was all about the Savior of our souls! Therefore, how could we NOT use this platform to glorify His name? Even in the face of what the world saw as a tragedy, God, in His sovereignty, saw as planned. Just as R.C. Sproul once said, "If there is one maverick molecule floating through the universe, then God is not sovereign!" We were told of several salvations through the ordeal of our son!

Meanwhile, we watched Jason's body decline. This is significant because he was strong and physically healthy. He worked out with weights in the garage at home every chance he could. He was on the high school football team, active in school, and active with friends from our church. He worked hard in the weight room at school. People noticed his work ethic in this area of his life. His friends nicknamed him Eugene "Boulder Shoulders." His strength served him well. He had thick thighs and strong arms, but it did not take long for him to begin to lose the muscle mass that he worked so hard for.

This gave us a new perspective on Isaiah40:6–8, "All flesh is grass, and all its loveliness is like the flower of the field. The grass withers, the flower fades, when the breath of the Lord blows upon it; surely the people are grass." It continues to be a reminder of how frail and temporary our physical bodies are. Each day was a challenge, but God measured enough grace for that day.

It really became overwhelming to grasp the outpouring of love, prayers, and assistance we received during that time. We saw God's grace in so many ways and were constantly reminded of God's grace and kindness in our lives. His body—the church—ministered to us on a daily basis. As well, members from both of our families were faithful to encourage and walk with us in so many ways. Coworkers visited as often as they could. Old and new friends from Facebook and a GoFundMe page were so generous and gracious. The community in which we lived rallied around us in tangible ways during this time as well.

During this ordeal in our lives, the Lord gave us a gift. Yes, a gift. We were able to be with Jason while he lay in the hospital bed. The doctor's indicated that Jason could likely hear us which led us to read as much Scripture as we could to him. The Lord led me to read Ephesians 2:1–10 to Jason often. God's Word is powerful. The fact that Jason was not conscious was no barrier for those powerful words. His Word does not return void and God uses it in mighty ways.

I prayed that the Holy Spirit would work in Jason's mind and in his heart as he lay in that hospital bed. Our pastors and elders prayed with us and prayed with him. They were faithful to give us guidance when needed. Ben and I each were blessed at separate times by him opening his eyes and giving us a response as they would perform the AGPAR test on him. It's so funny that it didn't happen when we were together—it was our own individual moment with Jason.

As we started the fourth week of Jason's hospital stay, the swelling in his brain was slowly coming down. He began to make enough improvements that the doctors wanted to change the way he was receiving oxygen. The procedure would make him more comfortable and it was important to remove the breathing tube from his throat and mouth. The procedure was scheduled for March 14. We were optimistic and excited that this might be the beginning of his road to recovery. As we made our way to his room, we were informed that they were not able to perform the surgery. His numbers had dropped too low. We were so disappointed. They said they would try again the next day. That would not be the case.

As the week went on, his lungs deteriorated. The doctor's and care providers—who were amazing—simply could not get his lungs to respond to treatment. It was a grueling week; Samuel, our older son, was involved in several long nights with Jason. Gabe, who had been largely cared for by family, friends, and church family, was brought in to see his brother as he lay in the bed almost lifeless. The week before Jason's death, March 17, is nothing that I can even describe. There are moments in that week that I am not sure that I will ever be able to put on paper or express to anyone other than my husband. They were so private and tender that God holds those in the palm of His hand and the tears from those times are "collected in His bottle" (Psalm 56:8).

During that week, each day revealed the fact that Jason was not able to recover from his injuries. As I write this there is still an element of disbelief. We quickly realized that the previous three weeks were not a recovery but a long goodbye to Jason. I cannot tell you how thankful I am that the Lord extended Jason's life for those four weeks. Every parent who has lost a child has a unique story. I often think of how blessed we were that Jason did not die instantly as some children do. Some parents lose their child in an instant. Some parents do not have the opportunity to say goodbye.

The evening that Jason died we were again surrounded by faithful family, church family, and close friends. Those that were not with us physically, we knew were praying for us and were with us in spirit. Our pastors ministered to us as we prepared for Jason's organ donation. That evening, Ben and I experienced something that few parents experience. In the early morning hours of September 1, 1999, we welcomed Jason into our family and in the evening of March 17, 2017, we said goodbye.

We know that God fully sustained our family through those weeks. He continues to do so as the sharpness of grief becomes a dull ache. God carefully unfolded a story of grace, mercy, kindness, and compassion to our family and the larger community through the death of our son, Jason. He used His Word to comfort us and Jason; he used His sovereignty to show us true peace; and He used His body, the church, to show us love that surpassed any human understanding.

How is it that we say God was kind to us when our son has died? God is always kind to us just by allowing us to continue to breathe. He gives us a measure of grace each day and we don't thank Him for it. What is the purpose of this life then? The first purpose is to glorify God. God had already been gracious to us by allowing us to have three healthy boys and we wanted to continue to give Him the glory. Our instinct as humans is to turn to despair, but when you glorify God you turn all things over to Him.

It became abundantly clear to us how important the gospel message was at this time and in all times. God's glory, the salvation of those whom He has called, and the message of Christ's death and resurrection were reinforced so lovingly by our great God through the Holy Spirit during this time of trial. God uses trials and temptations such as these to draw us to Him like no other time in the normal flow of life. We can look at the story of Job and his faithfulness as God allowed all of his possessions to be snatched from his hands. Or the teaching of Solomon in Ecclesiastes 7:1–2, where wisdom tells us that "the day of one's death is better than the day of one's birth" and "it is better to go to a house of mourning than to a house of feasting." We are taught so much more through trials than through any joyous time in our lives. First Thessalonians 4:13 instructs us to "not grieve as do the rest who have no hope." We place our hope in our Lord and Savior, Jesus Christ!

Messer Family ~ 2017

Jason Messer
September 1, 1999 ~ March 17, 2017

Our instinct as humans
is to turn to despair,
but when you glorify God
you turn all things over to Him.

HOPE & HELPS

Scripture we clung to on the hardest days/nights:
<u>Both:</u>
>Psalm 103; Revelation 22:1; Ephesians 2:1–10; Romans 1:16

<u>Ben:</u>
>Psalm 119 (emphasizes the importance of God's Word); Ephesians 1:3–14; Romans 8:26; Romans 8:38–39; 1Peter 1:3; 1Peter 4:12–13

<u>Stephanie:</u>
>Romans 5:3–5; Psalm 145:17–18; Psalm 54:4 (This was taped on my desk at work. There were many hard days at work because I had taken a new job. Between the overwhelming grief and the long, difficult days at work, I clung to this truth); Psalm 59:16; Deuteronomy 31:8 (during the last week of Jason's life)

Helpful things people did to minister to us:
- There were so many things that so many people did for us. It seemed we were helpless to do anything for ourselves in the beginning, so several people took over. If there was a need, someone filled it.

- Many people wrote down passages of Scripture for me to have on hand on note cards or slips of paper. And instead of keeping those hidden or put away, I pass them along to others who are going through a tragedy or trial.

- Someone helped me take notes when the doctors would talk to us.

- Food and meals were always good.

What you should NOT say to someone in a similar circumstance:
- "I know how you feel."

- "Let me tell you about something similar that has happened to me." This does not affect me like it does others that are going through loss. I expect people to say things that they think are helping but aren't really. I simply have sympathy for them and it can show me where they are spiritually so I know how I can pray for them.

Hymns or songs that comforted us:
<u>Ben:</u>
- *He Will Hold Me Fast*, Habershon/Merker

- *My Hope and Stay*, Norton Hall Band

- *Give Me Jesus*, African American Spiritual

- Books: I found great comfort and joy in so many books by Puritans and reformers.

Stephanie:

My song list is too long but I do have a couple of books that ministered to me in a great way after Jason died:

- *Stepping Heavenward*, Elizabeth Prentiss

- *The Path of Loneliness*, Elisabeth Elliott

- *Leaving Darkland*, Ed Wallen

- Quote by Charles Spurgeon that gave me great comfort:

  "When a tear is wept by you, do not think that God does not behold it. The Lord said: 'I have indeed seen the misery of My people in Egypt. I have heard them crying out because of their slave drivers, and I am concerned about their suffering. So I have come down to rescue them' (Exodus 3:7–8). Perhaps no figure of speech represents God in a more gracious light, than when He is spoken of as stooping from His throne and coming down from heaven to attend to the wants and woes of His redeemed people. How can we but love Him, when we know that He numbers the very hairs of our heads, marks all our paths, and orders all our ways?

  "When a tear is wept by you, do not think that God does not behold it, for 'You keep track of all my sorrows. You have collected all my tears in Your bottle. You have recorded each one in Your book' (Psalm 56:8). Your sigh is able to move the heart of Jehovah, your whisper can incline His ear unto you, your prayer can stay His hand, your faith can move His arm! Do not think that God sits on high taking no account of you. For the eyes of the Lord run to and fro throughout the whole earth, to show Himself strong on behalf of those whose heart is perfect toward Him."

The hope Jesus has given us through our loss of Jason:

Ben:

James 1:2–4 says that we should consider ALL things joy! That is inconceivable to this world! Then, as I look at the words of Solomon, who says it is better to go to the house of mourning than to the house of rejoicing, how can we worship a sovereign Lord in one breath and doubt what He is doing with the calling home of a loved one in the next breath? He simply causes us to grow in holiness. Our life is fleeting and eternity is forever!

Stephanie:

In Revelation 21:3–4 it says: "And I heard a loud voice from the throne, saying, Behold, the tabernacle of God is among men, and He will dwell among them, and they shall be His people, and God Himself will be among them, and He will wipe away every tear from their eyes; and there will no longer be any death; there will no longer be any mourning , or crying, or pain; the first things have passed away." Jesus is that provision for us on this side of eternity, but my greater hope will be the day when He comes again to abolish pain, tears, mourning, sin, and evil forever.

I Must Tell Jesus

Elisha A. Hoffman

The Lord is the one who goes ahead of you;
        He will be with you.
He will not fail you or forsake you.
    Do not fear or be dismayed.

Deuteronomy 31:8

Tears

Emily Curtis

Long ago there was a life I envisioned full of lighthearted joy
and the pattering of little feet. But my vision was not Yours, Lord.
So I shed tears. And you gathered them. And placed them in your bottle.

I wished for a body that was able and strong, running along shores
and dancing in the sunset. But You chose to have me walk a different path.
So I shed tears. And you gathered them. And placed them in your bottle.

My desire was to know the bond of love and live this life hand in hand with the one
You created for me. But You have deemed it good for me to travel alone.
So I shed tears. And you gathered them. And placed them in your bottle.

When my heart was overwhelmed with sorrow, and I ached for all I hoped this life
would be; when I felt unseen and my eyes were wet and weary from my tears
You gathered them. And You placed them in Your bottle.

Not one change of plans has startled You and You've never left me abandoned
or without hope. You gathered all the remnants of my broken dreams
and You have replaced them with all that is good in Your perfect wisdom.

For I do not have a Father who is distant from my grief.
You mourn with those who mourn and offer mind surpassing peace.

I will trust Your plans are for my good and You are acquainted with me most
intimately. Not a single tear I shed has gone unseen.
You have gathered them. And placed them in Your bottle.

You number my wanderings; Put my tears into Your bottle;
are they not in Your book?

Psalm 56:8

A JOURNEY OF FAITH

GILLIAN TOWNSLEY

*Dedicated to my husband. I couldn't have gone through this with anyone else.
You were strong when I was weak. You spoke truth when I thought lies. You showed me
light when I saw darkness. You are God's greatest earthly gift. I love you.*

It was my twenty-first birthday. Twenty-first birthdays are to be celebrated with much joy and zest for life. Mine was different. Of course, my family tried to make the day as special as they could considering the circumstances. As I sat trying to enjoy lunch at the very expensive restaurant that my father graciously took us to, all I could think about was the precious life growing inside of me. During my twenty-first year of life, I was being tasked by my heavenly Father to carry something beautifully, wonderfully, life-changing and gut-wrenchingly painful. The task of bringing Faith Isabella into this world, caring for her in a short but sweet life on this earth, and releasing her into the safe arms of God.

My pregnancy began normally, but as routine testing came back with concerns, we were referred to a perinatologist for additional testing. They confirmed that we were having a girl! I had always wanted a daughter, as I am the girliest of girls and could not wait to share in all of the mommy-daughter memories. He noted that he saw some issues with her head shape, growth, and hands, which he referred to as soft markers for a genetic condition called Trisomy 18. He encouraged us to do one more test to give a final result and we decided to go ahead with the test. Then came the waiting. Agonizing waiting.

When we finally got the call, we figured they would just tell us the results over the phone, but they asked us to come in. That's never a good sign. I can remember this day so vividly. The color of the sky. Eating breakfast in the car because we arrived too early. The arrangement of the chairs in the office. Looking at a magazine as I sat sitting in the waiting room. Waiting to be called. The genetic counselor running late because of traffic on the freeway. Her poor choice of words as she walked in rumpled and out of breath as we sat dry-mouthed and sweaty-palmed. "It's never good to be late on a day like today." That's it. It's confirmed. Trisomy 18. She sat down and I began to cry.

She said something but I wasn't listening. I then heard, "You have two options." My husband interrupted her firmly and said, "We have one option. We will be keeping our daughter." Then I just got up and left. I wanted nothing more to do with the coldness and harshness of that place.

Trisomy 18 is incompatible with life—60% of babies die in utero. Of the 40% that make it to full term, 90% of them die before the age of 1 and the average lifespan is three days. Three days. Is that all I will get with my baby girl? Will I even see her alive? If she lives longer, what will her complications be? The unknown was terrifying.

I began journaling my thoughts and prayers as a way to cry out to the Lord for help. Sometimes it was all I could do to make it through another day. By God's grace my pregnancy progressed normally and I made it to 37 weeks. At this visit my OB noticed that my baby was not getting enough blood flow and so he sent us home to pray over what decision to make in her birth process.

A normal delivery would be easier on me and spare me from possible future complications, but he did not think that she was strong enough to survive that type of delivery. A C-section was quicker, and could deliver her more safely and quickly, but it was major surgery and could even affect our future family. Neither option was a guarantee that she would be born alive.

We were so thankful for the wisdom and care of a loving, godly doctor We prayed and talked and my mother's heart just knew that I could not leave her in my womb knowing she was deteriorating. She was my child and we would do whatever it took to deliver her. Even if that meant one minute or no minutes with her. So, we prepared for a C-section. I wrote Psalm 23 on notecards to recite to myself as they prepped for surgery. I remember it like it was yesterday, holding those cards, cold, my hands and body shaking, the nurse tenderly helping me as I received my spinal tap. So scared, yet trusting that the Lord was holding me and Faith safely in His grasp.

On June 2, 2005, Faith Isabella Townsley was born. It was a beautiful, sunny, warm, Southern California day. John said, "She's crying, can you hear her crying?!" It was the tiniest little cry. It sounded like a kitten. So weak and so sweet. But she was alive and she was breathing! All 3 lbs, 1.9 oz. of her tiny, frail frame was fighting! Sweet relief.

The next few days were a blur. Family and friends visiting, a myriad of tests, learning how to care for her, and recovering from surgery. Some of the nurses didn't quite know how to handle our joy. They would pull my parents aside and ask them if we understood the gravity of the situation. It was a way for us to explain that YES! We did! We were just so grateful and thankful for this time with her. Our friends were sharing in that joy with us! My room was filled with flowers and gifts and visitors. They didn't quite understand but it was a way for us to share Christ with them through our hope even through the shadow of death. After a week in the hospital, we were going HOME!

We purposed to live a normal life with Faith for as long as the Lord allowed for us to have her on this earth. So, we played with her and dressed her up and took her to church and weddings and on trips and took pictures—all the normal things that parents do with their babies. She even went to a tea party with me! I knew that each day might be her last and that was scary. Living with that wasn't easy. There were many dark days and darker nights.

But God. He was so faithful to grow me and give me just enough grace for each day. Everywhere we went we had the opportunity to share our story. We were often met with questions and stares as she was the size of a living baby doll! At times this was incredibly difficult, and I just wanted a "normal" experience with a newborn baby. We were stopped once inside a Costco by a very inquisitive woman, and she boldly asked us if the hospital let us take her home! My first thought was one of sarcasm and I wanted to respond with "No, we stole her! Be sure to look for us tonight on America's Most Wanted." However, the Holy Spirit graciously took a hold of my words and I was able to kindly and calmly respond that, yes, they did let us take her home. Shockingly, she asked if Faith would be okay, would she live. Her brazenness was beyond my understanding. It hurt. I kindly but firmly said, "No, she would not be okay," and then I had to walk away before I broke down. I felt robbed. Robbed of the simple joy of taking my daughter out to the grocery store. The gawking eyes. The prying questions. Total strangers digging up pain when we were trying to enjoy a lovely day with our daughter. Every day, one day closer to her last.

Many of my days were filled with medical and therapy appointments. Trisomy 18 causes severe mental retardation and physical deformities, including heart and other major internal organ abnormalities. Surprisingly, Faith never suffered any of the dire issues that usually are the cause of death in these babies. She did have a small pin hole in her heart which began to close on its own. She also had a twisted bowel, which she underwent surgery to correct in October 2005, and did exceedingly well! However, she could not do many of the basic things newborn babies can do. She was fed through a nasal gastric tube, which later became a gastrostomy tube, which was placed during her bowel correction surgery.

She did not have the ability to smile or laugh or roll over. She was my perpetual newborn! Feeding time was sometimes very stressful. Faith and her daddy had this special bond. She loved him more than anyone. He could calm like no other could. All she had to do was hear his voice and she would quiet down immediately. I remember one afternoon she had pulled out her tube and it happened to be right around feeding time. She was screaming and I was frantically trying to gently thread the tubing down her throat. I tried and tried but could not get it all the way down to her tummy. I called John and he came to the rescue! He sweetly took her in his arms and at the soothing sound of his voice she stopped panicking. He was able to thread the tube and I was finally able to feed her. Daddy, our hero! Their bond was unforgettable and I will always treasure those precious memories.

The darkest valleys were walking through the whys. I was definitely learning to trust Him more through this path. I've never prayed more. I remember believing with my whole heart that the Lord could heal her if that was His will. Here is one of the many prayers that I wrote while crying out to Him with fear and love for my unborn baby. We had not decided on her name yet and this prayer seems a fitting foreshadowing of how the Lord would form her name in our hearts. "Oh Lord, help John and I to be strong! Help us to glorify You in our attitudes and actions. May we be a light to those unsaved around us. Help us to have faith and peace, knowing that You are in control. Grant us wisdom. Lord, I pray that this cup might pass from us. Be gracious and merciful unto us. Oh, Father God, give us our baby to live and thrive. May her life be long and glorifying unto You. Your will be done." Going through something like this at the tender age of 21 really shaped who I am today, and I am thankful for every minute of it.

Through it all, we enjoyed celebrating as many of the holidays we had with her including Thanksgiving and Christmas. We also had her announce to our friends and family that she was going to be a big sister in the spring of 2006! It was such a mix of emotions for me. On New Year's Eve, we decided to travel to John's family to celebrate the holidays with them. She had been fighting a cold but was doing well. I noticed that evening that her coloring seemed a bit off but just attributed it to the lighting of the store. Looking back, I know that was God's providential hand. In the early morning hours of January 1, 2006, we awoke to find our precious baby Faith perfectly at peace and resting in the arms of her Savior. We had the blessing of caring for her in this life just one day shy of seven months.

The day I dreaded for so long had finally come. Instead of the gripping fear that I had imagined, there was overwhelming peace. The words I was saying were not my words. The decisions I was making were not my decisions, and how I was carrying them out were not by me. The Holy Spirit was guiding me in every breath I was taking. I can vividly recall every detail like I was watching a movie in slow motion with an epic score playing in the background. Serene. Surreal. When the Lord says His grace is sufficient, this is what He means. He will sustain when you most need it. Moment by moment. Breath by breath.

The most painful memory I have was saying our final goodbye. When I had to release her from the protection of my warm arms over to a stranger. I knew at that moment I would never hold her again. I would never get to smell her sweet head or kiss her soft cheek. This was final. Nothing can prepare you for it. Picking out a casket. We chose pink. Deciding what to bury her in. A cream-colored dress with a delicate fur collar, cream tights, and satin shoes with a sweet bow on her head. At the cemetery, we laid her to rest in the peaceful baby garden, by a brook. I've often thought how glorious it will be when the Lord returns and all of those precious children fly to meet the Lord in the air! What a joyful day that will be!

In the days and months after Faith's passing, I had many deep waters to wade through, and many joys to celebrate. Wrestling with the fear and guilt of being pregnant while losing another child was a daily battle. I wanted my son, but I struggled with wanting my daughter more. How could I love him and still love her? Why couldn't the Lord have allowed her to stay? I wanted her back. I wanted her with me. I wanted him too. At times the pain and joy were so intertwined that I didn't know where one began and the other one ended. But once again the Lord loved me through it all and gave grace and kindness when I needed it most.

Since the Lord has taken Faith home, our family has continued to grow. The Lord blessed us with five handsome sons, whom we affectionately refer to as the Boybarians—Owen, Asher, Knox, Reichen, and Paxton. Though we have loved and enjoyed our sons more than anything, I once again wondered if I would ever have a daughter to hold in my arms. After many, many years of praying and many, many sons, the Lord kindly blessed with us a Valentine's Day gift, our daughter, Aria Felicity Hope. Her name has so much meaning for us. Before we knew of Faith's condition, we had planned on naming her Aria. One day while driving down the 5 Freeway in Los Angeles, John said "I just don't think that name fits her." I agreed and wondered what we could name her. He quickly said, "What about Faith?" Faith. It was perfect. When we found out we were having another daughter, we instantly knew we would use Aria and that her name had been saved just for her. Felicity means happiness and we have had much happiness with, and much hope for, both of our daughters. Hope for their salvation and their souls to be eternally with Christ forever. The Lord has answered our prayers in a different way than we ever imagined, but His ways are always good, and we will continue to set our joy and hope in the One who can do all things for the glory of Himself.

Although Faith's journey on this earth has come to an end, we still hear of those whom her life has touched. Those who we shared the gospel of Christ with because of her tender life. Other moms who I have been connected with, whose children also had or have Trisomy 18. Her life had purpose. Her life had meaning. God was glorified in and through her. Though the journey was painful and there were days I felt would be my last, I have lived and understand so deeply what Paul said to the Philippians to be true. "Indeed, I count everything as loss because of the surpassing worth of knowing Christ Jesus my Lord. For His sake I have suffered the loss of all things and count them as rubbish, in order that I may gain Christ and be found in Him, not having a righteousness that comes from the law, but that which comes through faith in Christ, the righteousness from God that depends on faith—that I may know Him and the power of His resurrection, and may share His sufferings, becoming like Him in his death, that by any means possible I may attain the resurrection from the dead" (Philippians 3:8–11). I am beyond grateful the Lord chose us to walk this path. May we never lose sight of the One who holds us fast on this Journey of Faith.

Gillian and Baby Faith,
the day Faith was born. June 2. 2005.

Faith Isabella Townsley
June 2, 2005 ~ January 1, 2006

John and Gillian Townsley
with their children

The Lord loved me through it all
and gave grace and kindness
when I needed it most.

HOPE & HELPS

Scripture we clung to on the hardest days/nights:
Lamentations 3: 22–23

Helpful things people did to minister to us:
- Brought meals.

- Brought groceries.

- Made items in remembrance of Faith: paintings, blankets, candles, shadow boxes, etc.

- Remember her birthday and always send a text or card—even after 15 years.

What you should NOT say to someone in a similar circumstance:
- "Let me know if you need anything." I couldn't even comprehend what I needed and even if I did, I wouldn't have wanted to ask. Just bring dinner, give a grocery or restaurant gift card, send money anonymously. Don't ask, just do. Just anticipate the needs and meet them. That will be a huge blessing.

- "Are you okay?" The short answer is no, we aren't okay. It's hard and it's painful. We aren't just going to bounce right back. We know that you want us to heal and feel better and that you are just concerned for our hurting hearts. But asking that question puts so much pressure on us to have the response that people think Christians are "supposed" to have. The Bible says that there is a time for mourning. That Jesus wept when Lazarus died, even though He knew He was going to raise him from the dead! Let us mourn. Mourn with us! Weep with us! Sit in the ash heap with us.

- "Why haven't I heard from you?" Feel free to text or call, but do not be offended if you don't get a response. There were days when I wanted and needed people and there were days when I just didn't have the strength. BUT, don't just stop. Grief is a long, hard process. There will be many hills and valleys they must walk through. The friendship may be one-sided for a while. Understand that and just be patient. We were thankful for every encouragement sent. Continue to pursue and love through the grief.

- "This is the Lord's will. Maybe this is better." We know this was His will. Everything the Lord does is for our good and His glory. That does not negate the agonizing pain and sorrow and sting of losing a child. Imagine yourself in that position. Choose your words carefully. The Lord's will can be pain-filled. His better can be our worst, but we trust him. Just be our loving friend.

- Forget about us and our daughter. Everyone gets caught up in the suddenness of death and we were overwhelmed with flowers, food, gifts, visitors, cards, and more. Suddenly that began to fade and people went back to their lives because they aren't living in that day-to day-grief. It became lonely at times. People don't want to even talk about your loved one for fear of making you hurt. But please remember them with us! We love talking about Faith! It is our joy to share about her life with anyone who will listen. It means so much to us that some still send texts or cards years later on her birthday and her home going date. She lived a short but meaningful life and it means so much to us that she left an eternal mark on the hearts of those who were blessed to know her.

Hymns or songs that comforted us:
- *Great Is Thy Faithfulness*, Chisholm/Runyan
- *My Jesus I Love Thee,* Featherson/Gordon
- *It Is Well with My Soul*, Spafford/Bliss
- *Be Still and Know*, Steven Curtis Chapman

The hope Jesus has given us through our loss of Faith:
The hope of heaven is so much sweeter knowing that we will be reunited with our sweet daughter. But even through the darkest of days when you feel like all around you is as black as night and you will never come through the other side, Jesus sees. He is the light that will guide you and the strength that will pull you through. And He is SO, SO good.

MY JESUS I LOVE THEE

William R. Featherstone

©MichaelKravchuk.com

Adniram J. Gordon

And there is no creature hidden from His sight,
but all things are open and laid bare
to the eyes of Him with whom we have to do.
Therefore, since we have a great high priest
who has passed through the heavens,
Jesus the Son of God,
let us hold fast our confession.
For we do not have a high priest
who cannot sympathize with our weaknesses,
but One who has been tempted in all things
as we are, yet without sin.
Therefore let us draw near with confidence
to the throne of grace,
so that we may receive mercy
and find grace to help in time of need.

Hebrews 4:13–16

You Are God

Emily Curtis

Lord,
Look upon my frail and weary soul,
Hold me in Your arms so that my heart may know
You are God.

Underneath Your wings,
Grant me refuge from the storm
When this world feels bitter cold, let your love, Lord, keep me warm
For You are God.

Remind me of Your faithfulness toward those who call You "Father"
You have shut the mouths of lions and parted mighty waters
For You are God.

Help me persevere, knowing I am weak
In my most fragile moments, it's Your strength my soul shall seek
For You are God.

My heart rests quietly in You and all Your perfect ways
Knowing Your plans are good and You have prepared each of my days
For You are God.

In the valley help me sing as You write out my story
You are my Savior, my Refuge, my King, so to You I will give glory
For You are God.

May Your steadfast love comfort me,
according to Your promise to Your servant.

Psalm 119:76

God's Comfort

Angelina Korotki

Blessed be the God and Father of our Lord Jesus Christ,
the Father of mercies and God of all comfort, who comforts us in all our affliction,
so that we may be able to comfort those who are in any affliction,
with the comfort with which we ourselves are comforted by God. —2 Corinthians 1:3–5

In December 2016, on the last day of my first semester at The Master's University, after the last exam was finished, my friend and I decided to relax and went to see Christmas lights and get some hot coffee on that very rainy and cold day. Riding along the highway we could hardly see the road due to that very heavy rain. Nevertheless, we bought our favorite hot coffee and went to the place where we were going to watch all the Christmas lights.

The rain became very heavy, so we decided to stop at the nearest coffee shop and wait until the rain stopped. After some time, we saw that the rain had almost stopped and we decided to continue our drive to see the Christmas lights. We had 15 minutes left until our destination, the rain had stopped, and it seemed that driving was not that dangerous anymore. We were listening to Christmas songs, drinking our coffee, and talking about our future plans. I remember watching little drops of rain on the car's windshield, an empty intersection, and a very bright traffic light.

The next moment, I opened my eyes and found myself laying in a hospital bed that was surrounded with my family who came all the way from Israel and Canada. Not understanding what was going on, I thought to myself, "What am I doing here? I have to go back to the university; I have to pass all of my exams."

Later on I was told that I was involved in a serious car accident and had been in the hospital the last three weeks. My friend who was in the car did not have any serious injuries because the car was hit exactly where I was sitting. I couldn't remember anything. I could not yet understand what was going on and what I would need to go through. I had Traumatic Brain Injury, many broken bones, and half of my body was paralyzed. I underwent serious surgery and would need to learn again how to walk, talk better, dress myself, and do countless everyday things. I had to go through physical therapy, occupational therapy, and speech therapy in order to get back to my normal life.

I did not know that my life would never be the same, I had to adjust to my new normal life. Many times I felt very discouraged while in the rehabilitation center. My life was divided into two parts—life before and life after the accident. My mom and dad were with me at the hospital and rehabilitation center every day. They would come in the morning and go back to their temporary home in the evening. Visitors from my church and university would come to see me and encourage me almost every day. My days were usually filled with different therapies and fellowship with people. My parents and I would always read the Bible and pray together before they had to leave me and go back to where they were staying.

Eventually, at the end of the day, I was in my hospital room alone with my heavenly Father. There were no visitors, no parents, no nurses, or doctors. I was laying in my hospital bed in a dark room, trying to scroll all the pictures on my phone (which was not easy because the left side of my body was not functioning well after being paralyzed), the pictures that I had from my first semester at Master's when my life was a "dream come true." My days were filled with new discoveries in a new country, new friends, constant fellowship, student life activities, music rehearsals and performances, and many other events. I had my life perfectly planned out but it all had changed in a moment. As I was laying in my hospital bed the song I Need Thee Every Hour would come to my mind very often. I remember laying in my bed at night, constantly repeating "Lord, I need You. ... I desperately need You every moment of my life. I need You so much."

I was surrounded with many people every day; nevertheless, I felt very lonely. I was in a very dark and deep ocean of loneliness. One day, I decided to sit down and write a letter to myself using some of my favorite Bible verses. I kept reading it when I felt discouraged. God's comforting Word is the biggest blessing! His Word is true and we can trust Him, always, in any situation!

> My dear child, I want to change your life. All the days for you were written in My Book before one of them came to be. I have planned everything for you from the beginning, I know that it might hurt and you will ask Me "Why Lord, Why?" But remember that blessed is the one whom God corrects. I wound and I also bind up. I injure but My hands also heal.

> My child, during this time you may feel tired and hopeless, but please remember that I am the Lord your God, Who takes hold of your right hand and says to you "Do not fear; I will help you."

> My child, do not be afraid but remember that in all things I work for good if you are My child and if you love Me. I want you to know that I will yet fill your mouth with laughter and your lips with shouts of joy.

> With love and care,
> Your Faithful Father

Sadly, I became distant with my friends because of the rehabilitation process. I was focused on becoming more like myself so that I would be able to continue my studies at The Master's University and continue singing (I am a music major and voice is my main instrument). I was born in a missionary family; I had always dreamed of being in a music ministry and serving God through my singing. I was always singing in choirs, worship teams, and singing solos in churches. I remember that very often I would go to my church during the week when there was nobody there. I would turn on all the microphones and sing for hours. I was sure that my voice would always be with me and I would always be singing in worship teams and solos. I love to sing so much; music has always been my passion!

But God had different plans.

After the accident, I lost my voice, and to this day it is not the same. I have been working hard in order to bring my voice back, but it hasn't improved much the last four years. After eight months of rehabilitation, I returned to my studies at the university but everything was different. I was different. I was not able to finish all of my homework well. My memory was not as good as it used to be. I couldn't have the same relationships with people around because I was always stressed about the fact that I was not the same anymore; I also had physical limits.

Doctors said my body began to "wake up" after the accident and I started having burning pain almost every day. There was no medicine that could help me. I remember one of the nights when I couldn't sleep because of the pain. It was a warm summer night, everyone was asleep except me. I was in my room with this burning pain in my body, in this room were only God, my pain, and me. I was laying on the floor and begging my God, "Lord, take this pain away, please … ." Then I was reading the Bible and listening to worship songs. As I was listening to worship songs and hymns, I was encouraged, distracted from the pain, my body relaxed, and I was finally able to fall asleep. The pain lasted for about eight months, some days it was strong, some days it was not.

Very often, my family and people from the university and church were trying to talk to me and encourage me, but I wouldn't open my heart to them because I did not want people to see the pain inside of me and feel pity. All I was thinking was: "My situation is too difficult; no one can help me because no one has gone through this situation. No one can understand what I am going through. I am feeling so lonely in this situation." I was often asking God, "Why Lord, why?" I was acting selfishly toward everyone around who loved me and wanted to help. I was feeling as if I were drowning in the deep and dark waters.

After some time, a woman from my church suggested that I read a book called Christ and Your Problems, by Jay Adams. As I was reading this book, God opened my eyes to this selfish attitude that I had. The author says in his book, "Christian, no matter how serious your present problems may seem, take heart! You are not alone. You have a sympathetic High Priest who can enter into all your problems, for they have been His problems too. He knows your heartache. He knows your sorrow. He knows your pain. He knows!"

The main Bible verse for this book is 1 Corinthians 10:13, where Paul says that there is no unique trial; you are not the only one who has gone through something like that. God is faithful; He will help you and provide a way that you can endure this trial. Jay Adams continues, "There's no trial into which God calls you that is beyond your ability to withstand, instead of saying "can't," you should say, "I can do all things through Christ who gives me strength."

At this point, I learned a very important lesson: God never gives us trials that we cannot overcome.

God was teaching me that He can use every trial for His glory and my good and to make me more like Christ through this difficult time(Romans 8:28–29). Slowly, God started to soften my heart; He surrounded me with His loving comfort. During this trial I found great comfort in God's promises and hymns. One of my favorite and most-comforting hymns became *It Is Well with My Soul*.

When peace like a river, attendeth my way,
When sorrows like sea billows roll
Whatever my lot, thou hast taught me to say
It is well, it is well, with my soul"

Another one is *Turn Your Eyes upon Jesus.*

Turn your eyes upon Jesus
Look full in His wonderful face
And the things of earth will grow strangely dim,
In the light of His glory and grace

I chose those hymns because when we turn to Jesus and focus on Him, then even the biggest waves of dark sufferings can't stop us from saying, "It is well with my soul!"

God was working on the process of my internal healing. Sometimes in this process I still fall into the ocean of discouragement, but God always raises me up again and again. I began to have bright hope in my heart; I understood that my situation was not unique; I am not the only one who has problems in my life and I am not alone. I started spending more time with other people, asking them about their trials and if there was any way I could be helpful or encouraging to them. God taught me that I can use my trial to encourage other people who are suffering. One of my favorite Bible verses became 2 Corinthians 1:3–5: "Blessed be the God and Father of our Lord Jesus Christ, the Father of mercies and God of all comfort, who comforts us in all our affliction, so that we may be able to comfort those who are in any affliction, with the comfort with which we ourselves are comforted by God."

I understood that I did not lose my musical dream. God slightly changed the direction of this dream. I can still be in music ministry and encourage discouraged souls with

Angelina's car after the accident ~ 2016

Angelina shortly after the accident

Angelina ~ 2020

God's promises and worship music. I want to comfort other broken souls with the same comfort with which I was comforted by God—through His Word and His promises that can be put into beautiful melody and serve as a balm for the soul. I often call it "music therapy from God's perspective."

Difficult times will come into our lives, but we must always remember that God's trials, which God sends, do not exceed our strength through Christ. They are not supernatural, but ordinary, human. In addition, we can take the lesson that God is faithful. He knows everything and is ready to help us at any time. When it seems to us that everything is falling apart in our lives and we can no longer keep going, God comes, comforts us, facilitates our trials, and He provides a way out of temptation.

HOPE & HELPS

Scripture I clung to on the hardest days/nights:
Isaiah 40:31; Isaiah 43:2; Romans 8:18

Helpful things people did to minister to me:
- When I was involved in the car accident, my parents came to the USA from Israel to be with me and they had nothing but my church, Grace Community Church, who showed us what it means to be a family in God. They gave my parents a place to live while I was at the hospital, as well as a car to use. People daily brought food, visiting and encouraging us.

- People were encouraging me with the hope and promises of God, and motivating me to work harder by telling me their own stories about their hardships or someone they knew and how God was helping them.

What you should NOT say to someone in a similar circumstance:
Personally, I do not love when people treat me with pity. It makes me feel miserable and discourages me from working hard.

Hymns or songs that comforted me:
- *Turn Your Eyes upon Jesus*, Lemmel
- *It Is Well with My Soul*, Spafford/Bliss

The hope Jesus has given me through this trial:
I know that Jesus is with me every step of this life. Some moments it can get SO hard and you do not know if you have enough strength to continue, but He Himself said, "I am with you always" (Mathew 28:20). And I can trust Him for sure! He will never leave me nor forsake me; He gives me strength for today and bright hope for tomorrow!

Turn Your Eyes upon Jesus

O soul, are you wea-ry and trou - bled? No light in the dark-ness you see?
Through death in - to life ev - er - last - ing He passed, and we fol - low Him there;
His word shall not fail you-He prom - esed; be - lieve Him, and all will be well;—

There's light for a look at the Sav - ior, and life more a - bun-dant and
o - ver us sin no more hath d - min - ion- for more than con-querors we
then go to a world that is dy - ing, His per-fect sal - va - tion to

free!
are!
tell!
Turn your eyes up-on Je - sus, look full in His won-der-ful

face, and the things of earth will grow strange - ly

dim in the light of His glo - ry and grace.

Helen Howarth Lemmel

*No temptation has overtaken you
but such as is common to man;
and God is faithful,
who will not allow you to be tempted
beyond what you are able,
but with the temptation
will provide the way of escape also,
so that you will be able to
endure it.*

1 Corinthians 10:13

Refuge

Emily Curtis

Although your world seems blanketed in sorrow,
I promise you, child, there is hope for tomorrow.
There are seasons in life for joy and for pain,
A season for crying and for laughing again.

I know that you feel overwhelmed and alone,
But my child, I see you and will not let you go.
I'll never leave you nor forsake you
So remember, when sadness may seem to o'er take you,
Nothing in this life can destroy you, dear friend,
For My plans are for you, there shall be hope in the end.

I will renew your youth like an eagle's and I shall restore your joy in full,
Find comfort in my wings for in your weakness, my strength will make you whole.
Hide yourself in the cleft of my strong and mighty rock,
Knowing I keep watchful care over each lamb in my flock.

I will rescue you from danger and from the sorrows life will bring.
I will place you on the dewy grass beside the peaceful stream.
My arms will wrap you tight; you are safe in My embrace,
And for each season of your journey, I'll sustain you by My grace.

God is our refuge and strength, a very present help in trouble.

Psalm 46:1

GREYSON AND GLORY

JESSICA COOK

For my thoughts are not your thoughts,
neither are your ways my ways,' declares the Lord.—Isaiah 55:8

My husband and I always said we wanted three children. Three was our number. We had been high school sweethearts, then married young in my second year of college. Matt and I always had a plan for our future together, even through the naivety of our young teen years when the mind sees nothing but hope and grand expectations for the impending future. Oh, how we thought we knew it all! We were going to take on this big world. And we'd do it together. Never anticipating that our plans were not God's plans.

Our first child was born on Camp Pendleton, where Matt was stationed with the US Marine Corps. We had planned to be career military, traveling the world together. But, of course, the arrival of a child changes your heart and desires forever. We chose to not reenlist but to come home instead so Bentley could grow up with family and a good church. Suddenly that plan to travel the world didn't seem as tempting anymore.

But we still had big plans! We were going to be the best parents we could be to little Bentley! I embraced this wholeheartedly as my plans and desires shifted from world traveler to stay-at-home wife and mother—and I loved every minute of it.

We went on to have a child every year for three years! We had Carson the next year and then Aubrey the year after that. Aubrey's pregnancy was a bit different, as she came a month early, but she was strong and healthy, so we counted ourselves blessed and never gave it a second thought. At that point, we had three children under three years old. We just adored having a home full of babies. Sure, it was hard having three in diapers, three waking up at night, three who couldn't do a single thing for themselves, but we still felt like we did just four years prior—"we've got this!" We had the overwhelming support of our families and church friends, although everyone joked they we may be going crazy! We had our three that we had always planned for, but our hearts and minds wrestled with the lack of peace in regard to closing that chapter of our lives. We made our plans long ago, however our plans are often not God's plans.

We soon became pregnant again, only to lose that one very early on in miscarriage. We cried, we grieved, but we still counted ourselves blessed as we looked at the faces of our three beautiful children. We continued on with the plans we had made for ourselves and started building a house to raise our family in. A few months later, we found out that we were expecting again. We were overjoyed and just starting to make our new plans in our minds for the arrival of our fourth child. I longed for that child in a way I never expected, given that we already had "our three."

The date of our first ultrasound came around and I decided to go alone, as Matt had to work very hard to support our young growing family. I laid there expecting it to be like any other routine ultrasound. I had no reason to believe anything to be amiss, but this time felt different. The ultrasound technician wasn't as talkative as I had known her to be in the past. "Maybe she was just having a rough day," I thought. She smiled and said,

"Just a second, I'll be right back." I sat there, still not expecting anything to be amiss, until the doctor walked in. She looked somber and spoke to me gently as she placed her hand on mine and said, "The ultrasound has revealed that the baby does not look as it should. We can tell from this that the baby has already passed away, and you will soon miscarry. I am so sorry. We will take bloodwork every few days to monitor that your body is doing what it should and doesn't need help removing the baby, since your body has not yet done that on its own naturally."

My heart sank. "Not again," I thought to myself as deep sobs welled up from the depths of my soul. The doctor gently hugged me. To this day I do not know her name, but she was the kindest doctor I have ever met. I've never forgotten the gentle compassion she showed to me in that moment. She hugged me gently as I sobbed. I'm sure most doctors don't do that.

Now I had the task of going home and telling Matt everything that had been conveyed to me, including the impending D&C (dilation and curettage) which would do what my body wasn't doing, removing the baby. However, that proved to be unnecessary as my body shortly after started to do just that. I continued to be monitored through bloodwork every few days to make sure the pregnancy hormone HCG was returning to normal. I don't remember how long that took, I think about two weeks, but they seemed like the longest weeks of my life. Again, we cried and grieved, then continued to move forward with our plans. Soon the day came to close on our newly built home. Matt and I went together; we did the paperwork and tried to be excited but the joy hadn't returned to my heart because the miscarriage was still so fresh. My wonderful husband, Matt, who is always trying to lift my spirits, suggested we make a date of it since my mom had the babies. So, we went to lunch right after. We sat there, mostly in silence, as I was trying to choke down some food. A task that had proven to be difficult in recent days. Then I received a call from the doctor. I was expecting a call telling me that my HCG levels were back to normal and that we could stop taking blood every few days. I had been increasingly frustrated with their lack of communication about my results. It turns out, that was for a reason.

I picked up the phone and heard the words, "Jessica, I don't know how to tell you this, but your HCG numbers are not returning to normal. It happens sometimes that the body stays confused and the numbers don't return to normal quickly. However, your numbers have been almost tripling every few days, which can only happen if there's still a baby growing in there. We need you to come back in. We think you had twins. The first did, indeed, miscarry, but there has to be another baby to explain these numbers."

I don't believe there is a word that adequately expresses my surprise and confusion. On the one hand, I was still grieving the loss of our miscarried child. On the other, I just found out that I am still carrying a child. It was a bittersweet feeling. I felt I could only be tentatively excited given the state of this experience.

Was this one healthy? Would I lose this one too? The next day I was in the doctor's office again for what was the most nerve-racking appointment I had ever been to. I tried taking deep breaths, so nervous that the stress would harm this potential "other" baby. Then there he was. Greyson. His picture was clear. He had a heartbeat. He looked untouched given the fact that he had been growing inside of a body so racked with stress and grief the last few weeks. Through all of the debilitating contractions I had experienced, he was still there. He was strong. We could clearly see on the ultrasound where the other baby had been, as there was a scar. The sight of that grieved my heart, however Greyson was still there on the other side, which gave me joy through my tears. They were fraternal twins. Because of the turbulent beginning to the pregnancy, I was closely monitored through the first trimester, but by the second trimester it was clear that he was healthy and all was well. No special monitoring was necessary. I was able to carry on as if everything was normal, because it was. He was growing and meeting every milestone. He was active and always kicking about. It was clear to me that he had quite a personality and I was so eager to meet him.

I continued being the wife and mom I had grown to be those last several years and had eventually stopped giving thought to those sad first weeks. Now my head was full of plans again. All was well! And then came the third trimester. At 32 weeks I began to have contractions. Immediately, those fears came flooding back to me. "Why was this happening? Was I being too active with my motherly duties of chasing babies?"

We rushed to the hospital. They pumped me full of medications to stop the contractions and gave me a steroid shot to help his lungs develop quickly in case of an early arrival. I don't remember how long I was there; the heavy medication made those few days a total blur. Then they sent me home to be on bed rest with medication to try to keep my body from going into early labor again.

It appeared that Aubrey coming a month early was not just a fluke. Having a baby every year had taken a toll on my body and I had rips and tears in the muscles that support the baby inside of me. My body was unable to support the weight of Greyson anymore. The bed rest gave him another two weeks to grow. I went into labor again, but this time it was for real.

He was coming six weeks too soon and there was no stopping my body. My broken body was failing me and my child. At the time of his birth, the neonatal intensive care unit was in the room, ready with ventilators and everything else they may need to help him survive this. I had never been so scared in all of my life. But then a miracle happened. He was born just a touch under five pounds, which was very large for a baby so young, and he was breathing on his own. Never once did they need to put him on a ventilator. He was a perfect version of what I experienced with my other children, only smaller.

He was perfect. My miracle child. The one I had longed for. The one I had prayed and begged God to save. He was here, he was perfect, and he was mine. Or so I thought. They kept us for an extra day but they permitted him to stay with me and not in the NICU because he was doing remarkably well. And then I went home with my beautiful miracle boy, knowing that this would be my very last baby. I treasured him in the knowledge that I would never again have another baby. Though he was small, he was mighty! Because he was a good size to begin with, the pediatrician's measurements put him at the first percentile on the full-term baby scale. He never ceased to amaze me. He was five pounds at that first visit. He gained very slowly for the first two weeks, only an ounce or two. Slow enough for the pediatrician to mention the possibility of him needing to be re-hospitalized, but then in that next week he gained sixteen ounces, which was almost unheard of, even by full-term standards!

Our other children, though young, cherished him deeply as our miracle baby and the very last addition to our family. They were always kissing him and teaching him new things like how to clap. He grew and grew, never getting sick, never having one health issue, and sleeping through the night by around seven months old. He met every milestone as if he didn't get the memo that he should be six weeks behind.

He never cried. It was the most remarkable thing. He was always happy and looking around. Extremely content with crawling around watching his brothers and sister play. He liked to walk anywhere where he could pull himself up to stand. He would do something silly and if it made you laugh, he would do it again to see you laugh once more and smile so big. I mean this kid had a personality! Funny, kind, quiet, content, sweet—perfect.

People made comments all the time about how happy he always was! At his one-year checkup, he had reached the ninety-seventh percentile for weight and height, tipping the scales at twenty-three pounds! He was bigger than our other kids ever were at this age! I was so proud of my big, beautiful boy. My miracle boy.

A few weeks went by, and, as any family has to deal with in February, sickness hit our household. Matt, Bentley, and Carson had all come down with something. One had strep, the others had the flu, but I was pleased that Aubrey, Greyson, and I were all fine. I tended to everyone and the boys seemed to be seeing the end in sight of their illnesses, so all was well. I put Greyson to bed that night and sang his favorite song:

"I love you Greyson, oh, yes, I do!

I love you Greyson, and I'll be true!

When you're not with me, I'm blue, boo hoo!

Oh, Greyson boy, I love you!"

He laughed and touched my face as he always did when I sang to him. Then I kissed all over his chubby face as I always did! I always loved that he never gave me trouble about kissing his face. Then I laid him down, he rolled over into his favorite spot, and didn't fuss as I left the room. I went to bed then woke up at 1:00 am to administer the older boy's medicine to keep their fevers in check and listened at Greyson's door, then went back to bed.

I woke the next morning and for some reason I just felt off. Not sick, just not as on top of it as I usually was. Matt, who had had stayed home from work that day because of his illness, said to me, "Are you ok? You seem quiet this morning." I responded, "Hmm, you're right. I don't know why though." I listened at Greyson's door but he was still asleep as he sometimes did. He was a great sleeper. I don't know why, but I took the other kids downstairs. I never went downstairs without all of the kids, probably due to their ages. We would usually wait until everyone was up and go down together. Maybe because Matt was home.

So I made a quick breakfast for the older three and went up to get Greyson. I quietly opened the door and smiled looking down on him sleeping on his tummy in his favorite spot. His arms stretched over his head with his little fingers curled around the top edge of the mattress. I stroked his back softly, but he did not stir. I started to feel a little panic rise in my heart and I grabbed his arm to turn him over. But I couldn't move his arm.

In that moment I knew. I turned his stiff lifeless body over and pulled him onto the floor, his arms still frozen above his head and his beautiful face, blue and contorted into a face so horrifying that it still haunts my nightmares. He was frozen, as if pushed up against glass. But that was my son, and I was truly terrified at the scene I was looking at but conflicted as I felt the greater urgency to hold my son.

I screamed for Matt who, thankfully, was home that morning and just in the other room. With shaking hands, I tried to perform CPR. Some irrational part of my mind told me that if I could just get him to breath, the color and the softness would return to his body, but I was wrong. Matt dialed 911 and I remember him saying, "Please help, my son isn't breathing." He put the phone down on the floor and started doing CPR himself, as he had learned in his military and EMT training, then told me to pick up the phone and talk to them until they arrived.

I don't know how much time passed between all of this, as I blacked out for bits and pieces. All I know is that by the time I got the front door open, the EMTs and police were running up to the house. I ran upstairs, they followed, just shortly behind. I kissed Greyson's head one last time, because I knew from Matt's EMT training that once they got there, I wasn't going to be able to touch him again. When a baby dies, the police have to investigate. So, the moment they enter the room, everything is considered evidence. Even my son.

I kissed his head quickly one last time in his own room, then was gently helped up by an officer. I collapsed into his arms as I blacked out. I was awake, my mind has just blocked out moments. Somehow my mom was called to take the kids, so they were out of the house shortly after. The next thing I remember was the deep throbbing pain in my soul that poured out my eyes as I cried and screamed, "God help me!" I remember being held by my dad. Somehow, he, my pastor, my brother, and sister-in-law had been called too. My brother and sister-in-law didn't know what to do, so they simply put away the toys that were strewn around my living room. I don't know how long I sobbed in my newly built kitchen, but I remember throwing up in the sink. And I vaguely remember screaming, "Where is my baby!?" And, "What am I supposed to do now?" As the absence of his weight in my arms felt overwhelming. It still is.

I don't remember those next few days, other than going back to the house for a few minutes to pick out his funeral clothing. I chose some pajamas with little yellow dump trucks on it that I loved and a striped hat, as I was told was necessary for him, given the autopsy. I remember opening the fridge, picking up his sippy cup and holding it to my chest and sobbing. He had just learned how to use a straw and he was so proud to have a cup like his older siblings. It was still full of his formula.

A few days later, I was sitting outside of the funeral home with Matt, afraid to go inside. Scared to my core to see what he may look like. The last image of him, still seared into my brain, turning my life into a living, breathing nightmare. But I did go.

Matt and I went alone for the first hour, then family was to come after our time. I slowly walked up to the toddler-sized casket and saw him. And he was beautiful. He looked like himself. The funeral director asked me if I wanted to hold him. I didn't know that was an option. I eagerly said yes, and I held and rocked him for two hours. The last two hours on this earth, holding my perfect miracle baby boy. My big, beautiful boy.

After those two hours, I wrapped him in the blanket I had recently made for him and tucked him into his casket. As if saying good night for the last time. We went to the gravesite and all I remember was slipping out my seat and sitting on the ground with my hands placed on the casket. I don't remember anything after that until the funeral.

We opted to do the funeral later that day, after his burial, at the recommendation of our pastor. I remember insisting to speak. I wrote an open letter to Greyson. Telling him that I loved him and that this wasn't the end. I would see him again. Telling him all the things I wished so deeply I could have conveyed to him, given the chance. At the conclusion of the service, we sang *It Is Well with My Soul*. With lifted hands through the deep groaning of my heart, though my legs wouldn't hold me, I sang it with the little energy I had left in the body that had grown weak from days of lacking food. Even now, two and a half years later, if we sing that song in church, I still go right back to that moment.

I never lived another day in that beautiful house that we built. The PTSD (post-traumatic stress disorder) kept me from being able to return except for once. I went by myself. I hadn't been there for months, but I went, unloaded the dishwasher that was full of clean dishes and took out the full load of laundry that I had left in the dryer. It was full of Greyson's clothes. Then I laid on the floor of Greyson's room and cried as hard and as loudly as I needed to. The whole time I kept hearing him talking. Babbling and hitting the wall with his hand like he always did when he woke. I knew it wasn't real, but the mind is a powerful thing. It sounded real to me. I never returned. Yet the sound of a baby crying and the smell of formaldehyde stuck with me for many more months.

My other children were plagued with many tears and night terrors. For over a year they would scream and cry in fear and anxiety if I left the room without telling them, fearing that I had disappeared like their brother did. There one moment, gone the next. They were too young to explain that they should be "anxious for nothing." At any rate, I wasn't the one who could be teaching them that lesson at that moment. I was still paralyzed by fear if they overslept or left my sight for even a moment. Some regressed back to peeing the bed because of their trauma. Others were breaking out head-to-toe in hives because of the immense stress on their little bodies. Their hearts were shattered, similar to mine. And I was helpless to take it away from them. One child had died, and the others were immensely suffering. And I was helpless to do anything about it.

Once Greyson passed, my health fell apart. All of ours did for a while. We were all plagued with chronic infections as the stress and grief suppressed our immune systems and the antibiotics couldn't work without our body's help. Eventually everyone else got better, but not me. I was diagnosed with an autoimmune disease. Even deepening the feeling of loss as sometimes I was unable get out of bed or even breath due to my severe muscle fatigue. I've spent days in the hospital because of my inability to draw breath. I have had to grieve the loss of, not only my son, but the woman I used to be.

I am no longer the woman I used to be. I see the world differently; I think differently; I act differently. I am different. And there were some days, not too long ago, that I have cried over the death of the ambitious, blissfully ignorant woman I once was. The woman with plans to be a world traveler. The woman who didn't know what it was like to live in a world where her baby was dead. The woman who was charismatic and enthusiastic and somehow kept the house clean and kept up well with the life of having four kids under four years old. The woman who had every intention and ambition to homeschool, yet my health and heart made me unable to do that, so my kids are in school now. Something that was not in "my plan." I liked her better. And I miss her. But even in that, God is gracious and faithful. If I hadn't gone through all of this, I wouldn't be writing to you. Ministering to you. Relating to you. God has made me who I need to be, for you.

Looking back, God's hand is so apparent in so many things. Even in the depths of pain, there is mercy. Why did I take the kids downstairs that morning before getting Greyson up? I still don't know, but if I hadn't, they may have witnessed all of this unfolding instead of being downstairs blissfully ignorant as they ate breakfast. Why did our new house take so long to sell in the height of the real estate market? I don't know, but it allowed the right couple, who are both nurses, to buy our house. The right couple who didn't mind the history and just happened to be friends with my sister-in-law who is also a nurse. No one knew the connection until later. Why couldn't we find a new house for so many months? I don't know, but if we had, we wouldn't have found this house, which was "for sale by owner" and had just put up the sign. This couple had just upgraded many things in the house, intending to stay, only for their grandson, who was a twin, just like Greyson; the fourth child in his family, just like Greyson; to pass away unexpectedly in his sleep—just like Greyson. They were selling their house to be near their daughter, who had just lost her son. Who was just like us. That is the hand of God. This house wasn't even listed anywhere online. Just a sign in the yard that we happened to pass on the way to another house we were going to view. But if we had sold our house sooner, and bought another house sooner, this would not have happened. God blessed two Christian families. He blessed us to get this wonderful house, which had just been upgraded, and them to sell the house they had built twenty-five years earlier to someone they cared about and knew what they were going through.

God is gracious, even in the depths of sorrow, even when your whole world is so devastatingly crushed and torn apart at the seams. When all the grand plans you had for your life come crashing to your feet, He is sovereign. He gently, lovingly picks you up with the shattered pieces of the life you thought you would have, and shapes it into something new. "'For my thoughts are not your thoughts, neither are your ways my ways,' declares the Lord" (Isaiah 55:8).

My plans for my life were never God's plans, but I know that God is faithful and I know that He loves me. He loves me so much that He CHOSE to give his son to die for ME. And his death wasn't the least bit peaceful. Choosing such debilitating pain and sacrifice on the behalf of a people who sin against him every day is beyond my ability to understand or fully comprehend. THAT is love. "Are not two sparrows sold for a penny? And not one of them falls to the ground apart from your Father's will. But the very hairs of your head are numbered" (Matthew 10:29).

A.W. Tozer said, "While it looks like things are out of control, behind the scenes there is a God who hasn't surrendered His authority." He's right; God has not surrendered His authority. There is a purpose to our pain. There is a greater plan. Today, I live in a home that is five minutes from my church, my family, and my in-laws. My three oldest kids are ages seven, six, and five now. They are in school and thriving. They love it. We openly talk about Greyson in our home and the kids' teachers know about Greyson, allowing the kids to never feel like they can't talk about him. The night terrors and anxiety in my children are gone. They enjoy helping me decorate "Greyson's place" with freshly planted flowers and tend to his tree.

The Lord brought a new healing option to me for my autoimmune disease and my health is improving every day, to the point where I see glimpses of that former woman coming through. My marriage is stronger than it has ever been, and I can laugh again without feeling guilt for smiling in a world where my son is absent. Some people have come to us asking, "How can you be so OK?" And we tell them it's because, this is not the end. We know the final chapter and God wins. And I belong to him. I will see and kiss my beautiful baby Greyson again. Not today, but someday. I rest in the assurance that I need not worry about him ever again because I know where he is, and I know he is cared for. Nothing in this life is promised. It can all be taken away, but when it does, God is still on His throne, and He remains. He is my only promised constant. He is my anchor and my strength. This is not the end.

"Though He brings grief, He will show compassion, so great is His unfailing love" (Lamentations 3:32).

"I love the Lord, because He has heard my voice and my pleas for mercy. Because He inclined His ears to me, therefore I will call on Him as long as I live. The snares of death encompassed me; the pangs of Sheol laid hold on me; I suffered distress and anguish. Then I called on the name of the Lord: 'Oh Lord I pray, deliver my soul!' Gracious is the Lord, and righteous; our God is merciful. The Lord preserves the simple; when I was brought low, He saved me. Return, O my soul, to your rest; for the Lord has dealt bountifully with you. For you have delivered my soul from death, my eyes from tears, my feet from stumbling; I will walk before the Lord in the hand of the living" (Psalm 116).

God is gracious,
even in the depths of sorrow,
even when your whole world
is so devastatingly crushed
and torn apart at the seams.
When all the grand plans
you had for your life
come crashing to your feet,
He is sovereign.
He gently, lovingly picks you up
with the shattered pieces of the life
you thought you would have,
and shapes it into something new.

Bentley, Carson, Aubrey
and Greyson Cook ∽ 2017

Jessica holding Greyson at
the funeral home ∽ 2018

Greyson Lee Cook
January 21, 2017 ∽ February 27, 2018

HOPE & HELPS

Scripture I clung to on the hardest days/nights:
Psalm 16:8; 31:7; 34:18; 56:8; 116:1-19; 138:3; Joshua 1:9; Isaiah 25:8; 40:8; 41:13; 43:2; 46:4; Lamentations 3:32; Ecclesiastes 3:11; Proverbs 3:5-6; Matthew 5:4; 10:29; Jeremiah 29:11

Helpful things people did to minister to me:
- My closest friends said nothing and just sat with me in silence; not requiring anything from me. Even speaking was too heavy of a burden for me at the time.
- Taking care of meals for my family because cooking was not possible for me at the time.

What you should NOT say to someone in a similar circumstance:
Do not try to bring up the loss of anyone or anything else to say that you understand. Losing a parent, grandparent, or pet will never be similar to losing a child and you absolutely do not understand. Same goes for "almost" losing your child. I have lived through miscarriage and the loss of a child. I have lost grandparents, pets, and even "almost" lost my son Carson earlier in his life. The pain is not equivalent. Don't try to say you understand unless you have lived with the kind of child loss that involves a child that you knew, bonded with, and grew to deeply love.

Hymns or songs that comforted me:
- *Though You Slay Me*, Shane&Shane
- *Even If*, Mercy Me
- *It Is Well with My Soul*, Spafford/Bliss
- *Oh My Soul*, Casting Crowns
- *Thy Will*, Hillary Scott
- *Homesick*, Mercy Me
- *More than Anything*, Natalie Grant
- *The Sweetest Gift*, The Piano Guys, ft. Craig Aven

The hope Jesus has given me through my loss of Greyson:
The hope that I will see Greyson again, and a disconnect from this world. I no longer see the world the same way. Pain and sin are more apparent. I look forward to and long for the day when Jesus returns and rids the earth of sin and evil and death. I long for heaven, the absence of sin, the absence of pain. He has given me hope that no matter how bad it gets for me here, He will sustain me until He calls me home. Then I'll get to live for eternity with Him.

The King of Love My Shepherd Is

Words: Henry W. Baker

©MichaelKravchuk.com

Music: Irish Melody

I will rejoice and be glad in Your lovingkindness,
because You have seen my affliction;
You have known the troubles of my soul,
and You have not given me over
into the hand of the enemy;
You have set my feet in a large place.
Be gracious to me, O Lord, for I am in distress;
my eye is wasted away from grief,
my soul and my body also.

Psalm 31:7–9

Heaven

Emily Curtis

Oh, when I'm free to sin no more,
When my feet walk the paths of celestial shores.
No longer a need for moon or sun,
When all is illumined by the Glorious One.

What joy when my faith shall be made sight,
When I'll no longer weep or be filled with fright.
When my weary body finds rest, is whole;
When my loving Father welcomes me home.

What wondrous things my eyes shall see,
Precious stone gates and golden streets.
Flowing before the throne of "I Am,"
Is the River of Life afforded me by the Lamb.
And on the side of this crystal sea,
Is the Tree of Life filled with healing leaves.

Free from the Curse; face to face with my Lord,
Worshiping Him purely forevermore.
Oh, what a glorious day that shall be,
When I call Heaven "home" for eternity!

And He will wipe away every tear from their eyes; and there will no longer be any death; there will no longer be any mourning, or crying, or pain; the first things have passed away. … and the city has no need of the sun or of the moon to shine on it, for the glory of God has illumined it, and its lamp is the Lamb.

Revelation 21:4, 23

His Way Is Perfect

Chris McDowell

Numb. That is the only word I can use to describe how I felt. The neurological ICU waiting room was full of my husband's coworkers and family friends from church. Word had spread quickly in our small military community of the crisis. I was standing in the hospital waiting room in Heidelberg, Germany, with our close family friend who is a native German. My husband, Mark, had been taken back for an angiogram less than 30 minutes prior. The test was to have taken at least an hour. Yet less than 30 minutes had passed and here was the doctor explaining something to Thomas. My conversational German was not good enough to follow his words.

Mark had collapsed playing basketball after having been on call at the hospital the previous night. He was rushed to the German university hospital since our military one was small and not as well equipped for a major cardiac event, which is what they thought they were dealing with at first. I had been running errands for Mark and was then picking up two college-age girls we had sponsored to come help in the church ministry there in Heidelberg. The girls came out from their work shifts and said that my oldest daughter had called and said that military police had come to the apartment looking for me and that a military chaplain was on his way to where we were. I was asked not to leave.

My mind starting racing, but I quickly surmised that they wanted me to be with them to tell my husband that something bad had happened to his mom. Her health had been declining and I was sure that must be what was taking place. When the chaplain, along with one of Mark's coworkers and her husband arrived shortly thereafter, I found out that Mark had collapsed, and they were concerned about his heart. He was just shy of 42 years old, but I didn't think it could be his heart. He had worn a Holter monitor for a couple of medical studies while he was in medical school. They always commented on his great heart condition. Mark was a very passionate and intense person. He played basketball with that intensity. It was August 27 and very warm and humid; I told myself that he just overdid it and probably got overheated.

When we arrived at the hospital , I saw a soldier with whom we went to church. I asked him what he was doing there and he informed me he was the colonel's driver. I was shocked that the colonel, who was our hospital commander, had been rushed over. As soon as I entered the waiting area, the colonel and his second in command began to explain to me that there was concern that Mark had suffered a ruptured brain aneurysm. I felt the full import of that news when the colonel informed me that he had already called Washington, D.C., and a medical board was being convened at that time in order to medically retire Mark. Numbness began to creep in as I tried to take in this information. I could not even see him because they were getting ready to take him for the angiogram. The colonel's second in command had been our family physician at one point and was a family friend. He made calls and assured me that close family friends were with our five children who ranged in age from six to fifteen.

The chaplain sat down with me and told me that he had seen some of the scripture verses framed on our walls when he had gone to the apartment. He asked about our beliefs. I told him that Mark and I were both born again believers and believed that

God was in control of all. He smiled somewhat sadly and said that made his job a lot easier. People were all around and everyone looked scared. I sat there and prayed. I asked God to give me grace to deal with what was ahead. I remember telling God that I didn't know how to pray. I did not want to petition Him for something that was against His perfect plan. I just kept asking over and over in my heart for God to help me to accept His plan. Everyone stayed close by in the waiting room. I was not allowed to be alone at all—even to go to the restroom—someone had to accompany me.

When our family friend, Thomas, arrived, he stepped in to help navigate the German system. When the doctor came out and walked straight over to me, Thomas introduced himself. They spoke briefly and then the doctor looked at me and said, "I am so sorry." Thomas explained that Mark had a brain aneurysm that had ruptured. The bleeding was so massive that they could not even get the contrast to go into the brain. That was why the test was cut short.

When tragedy strikes there is no "pause button" to allow you to absorb the grief. Life keeps moving forward, dragging you along whether you are prepared or not. Circumstances were suddenly forcing me to make decisions while my heart and mind screamed, "NO." What was I going to do? How was I going to tell the kids? I just kept praying in my heart, "Please God, help me." I thought of Romans 8:26, "Likewise the Spirit also helps in our weaknesses. For we do not know what we should pray for as we ought, but the Spirit Himself makes intercession for us with groanings which cannot be uttered." Family friends from church offered to pick up the kids and bring them to the hospital. There are no words to describe hearing the heart-wrenching cries of your children after being told that their father is going to heaven or stand with them at his bedside while they say their goodbyes.

I felt such a weight of responsibility. We had been teaching our children about God for years. If I could not live out my Christianity through this tragedy then how could my kids ever believe that the Bible was true?

In the midst of all of this, I was being asked all kinds of questions. So many things had to be decided. We were living in Germany. We were supposed to be moving back to the states in a year, but it hadn't been decided where we were going. Not only were we dealing with this tremendous loss, but we were living in a foreign country and did not have an established home base.

One of the ways God provided for us was the colonel petitioning for Mark to be medically retired. This gave us many benefits that would be such a blessing in the years ahead. Additionally, the colonel asked me who I might want as our casualty assistance officer. This was supposed to be an active-duty individual who had to be equal or higher rank to Mark. My thoughts were so jumbled I could not even think. I looked across the hospital bed at the colonel's second in command, the man who had been our family physician, and heard myself saying, "Gordy, could you do it?" He quickly responded saying, "I was hoping you would ask." The colonel explained that "Gordy," Dr. Gordon Miller, would be immediately relieved of his responsibilities and sent to a briefing. His responsibility the next few weeks would be to escort the kids and I everywhere and assist me with navigating through all the tasks and decisions that had to be accomplished. He even escorted us back to the states and stayed until after the funeral.

We left the hospital that night surrounded by many friends from church and work. Mark was being taken off sedatives in order for the medical staff to perform two separate EEGs (electroencephalograms) the next day. They told me his organs would begin shutting down. I would be returning early in the morning with Mark's living will and medical power of attorney papers. I had begun making necessary phone calls from the hospital, but as soon as we got home the calls continued. Germany is 6–9 hours ahead of stateside time. As word quickly spread, our phone rang almost nonstop all hours of the day as friends and family rapidly moved to start helping in any way they could.

I slept very little that night. Between phone calls and dozing, I lay in the dark talking to God. I kept hoping I would wake up and find that this was all a bad dream or a mistake. Looking back, I can see God's hand throughout my life laying the groundwork for the path He had for me. When I was born, it was quickly realized that something was wrong with my left eye. The specialists told my parents that it would be a miracle if I ever had sight out of that eye. I had a godly great aunt who greatly influenced my life. One day she told me that when my parents were given that news, she prayed and asked God that if He had a special purpose for my life that He would give me sight in my left eye. While it is much weaker, I do have sight in my left eye. My aunt always told me that my eye was God's special mark. Growing up, when being ridiculed or asked what was wrong with my eye, that story always brought me comfort. When I experienced a trial, I would remember that God was in control.

Now I was facing the biggest crisis I had ever faced in my life, and I was also responsible for our five children. Did I really believe what I had talked about for much of my life or was it just words? A few weeks before Mark's collapse, we had been lying in bed one night, talking and sharing. I had told Mark that I felt like life was so hectic, that I was just living my Christian life on autopilot. I expressed to him that everything was so rushed that I was not getting time to stop and really listen to God in my heart. While my outward actions exhibited Christian behavior, I felt I was missing that close communion with my heavenly Father.

Mark as always was an encouragement and I also know that he was praying with me that God would help me find the balance. Little did I know that God was already preparing my heart in order to rely on Him. In the days ahead, the truths that I kept finding myself saying to myself and others over and over again were the absolutes that I knew about God. Asking why was not going to help. Even if I knew why, it wasn't going to make me feel better. Thinking about all the what-ifs wasn't going to change anything. I had to cling to what I knew was truth, no matter what the circumstances. God loves me, God never makes a mistake, and He always does what is best. These truths are constant, never changing, and they are what I have clung to since that day.

Mark was taken off of life support the following afternoon. Since it was heading into Labor Day weekend, all the paperwork processing would be slowed down. I was told that I could head straight to the states but it might be best to stay in Heidelberg longer, where the military community knew us well and everyone was so willing to help with all that needed to be decided. I chose to stay. In reality I did not want to leave Germany with Mark's body still being processed. I knew he was present with his Lord and his body was just a shell, but I just didn't want to leave before his body did. Because it was an unexpected death, the army intelligence service still had to conduct a formal investigation. This process required that I had to undergo an interview. I was escorted and was treated kindly, but it was heart-wrenching to have to sit and answer investigative questions without breaking down. Much of the other paperwork was given to Gordy and he would bring it to me to deal with so I did not have to go to so many offices. When I did have to go in person, I was escorted. The military community held a beautiful memorial service in Heidelberg before we left and another was held at an outlying clinic after we were gone. The auditorium was packed and we were there for a long time afterward while everyone filed by and expressed their love and condolences.

All of the assistance was such a blessing, but God did not totally wrap us in cotton wool and buffer us from anything else. While the military would be moving our things back to the states, that process would take a few months. Anything that I felt we would need soon would need to be packed and mailed. Friends and neighbors descended on our apartment for several days. Some helped pack and sort. Others took the kids on an outing or to spend time with friends. When all the boxes were ready, a few ladies helped load our van and other vehicles to take everything to our base post office.

I walked in with my paperwork, which were orders stating we were being relocated to the states due to the death of the service member. A postal worker instructed us to bring the boxes in and stack them along the wall; once they were all in then I was to get in line to process them. When I got to the front of the line I found myself face-to-face with the one postal worker who was known for being gruff. I could tell he was not happy. I laid the orders down in front of him. He appeared to read them and then he proceeded to sternly reprimanded me for not calling and making an appointment to ship so many boxes. I apologized and told him I was not aware that I could have made such arrangements. He continued to grumble and make remarks while starting on the boxes.

The post office was full and people were watching, but I could tell some didn't know what to do even though they knew me and the circumstances. All of a sudden a woman came up to me and introduced herself as the colonel's wife and told me how sorry she was for our loss. She wanted to know how we were doing and did we need anything. We spoke briefly and after she walked away the postal worker asked me what had happened. In my heart I had so wanted to lash out at this man, but God stilled my tongue that day. Could I live out what I had said I believed? Instead, I pointed again to the orders, specifically the line that said "due to death of the service member." That man suddenly became my best friend. He was so horrified at how he had acted that he couldn't be nice enough or help enough. I tell this story because I think it is important to note that while God protects and provides, the tests and trials will still come. God provides grace moment by moment as it is needed, but we need to rely on Him.

Help came in many forms over the next few days, weeks, and months. Our neighbors came and asked for the keys to our vehicles. After finding out that I did not plan on shipping them back, they said they would take care of the sale of both the car and the van. They had both sold in less than a week. One of those same neighbors was a JAG (military, Judge Advocate General's) lawyer. He came over, reviewed all my legal papers, discussed any updates I needed, and returned with everything updated and then notarized my signatures. One couple with whom we were very close, came and stayed with us so we weren't alone. Once again, our neighbors stepped in and handled the military packers and movers after we left. Stateside, friends and family were instrumental in helping with funeral arrangements, short-term housing for us, finding a vehicle, and helping unpack when our belongings arrived.

After the funeral, and everyone began to return to their normal lives, we began to feel the true effects on our day-to-day life. Mark was not just gone on a long trip. We had moved. We had a new home. We had to start a new life, and he was not coming back. While I did not think of turning anywhere else but to God in this crisis—because I had no idea what to do—I did not do well with "small" upsets. Getting sideswiped by a careless driver only to find out she gave false insurance information put me into tears. Where was God? Having military paperwork—which clearly stated "service member deceased"—returned with a stamp that said, "needs to be signed by military service member" had me tersely asking a clerk on the phone how I was supposed to get my dead husband's signature? Mark and I used to say the hardest thing about marriage was what you find out about your sinful self. Well, I was quickly finding that I seemed to rely on God more easily for the trial of Mark's death than I did for the every day hiccups I faced following. I had to learn to rely on God, for every big and little detail in my life..

So many people wrote letters, shared verses, tapes, and books. Two books in particular impacted me greatly in those first few weeks. *When God Doesn't Make Sense* by James Dobson and *The Path of Loneliness* by Elizabeth Elliot. God had not changed and He had not moved away from me. His absolutes were still true. God loves me, He never makes a mistake and He always does what is best. When nothing else made sense, I had to lean on what I knew to be true. Whether I understood or felt loved, I had to trust what is true. A few months after returning to the states I was introduced to a song that quickly became my heart cry. Music has comforted me so many times during tests and trials. These words ministered to me in profound ways.

His Way Is Perfect, The Wilds

When my way seems dark and dreary and the future I don't know,
My heart feels so empty as the tears unending flow.
When my heart breaks with sorrow and a tempest fills my soul,
This one thing I know for sure: my God is in control.

His way is perfect, His way is perfect.
Though I don't understand His wise and loving plan,

His way is perfect. His way is perfect.
Take my life and make a vessel purified.
God makes no mistakes, His way is best.

When the toils of life are come and my heart is worn with care,
I faint 'neath the burden of a cross I cannot bear.
When the joy has departed from my sorrow-stricken soul,
This one thing I know for sure: my God is in control.

His way is perfect, His way is perfect.
Though I don't understand His wise and loving plan,
His way is perfect. His way is perfect.
Take my life and make a vessel purified.
God makes no mistakes, His way is best.

That song sums it up so well. I can't say that I have glided through these past 23 years. I made so many mistakes as a single mom. Independent decisions are so scary. I still miss Mark every day. He was my best friend, my confidant, my iron sharpening iron. Part of my heart went with him. I still do wish him back, but not at the expense of going against God's will. I was blessed to have had sixteen-and-a-half years with him. I can't say that I am thankful for his death, but I can say that I am thankful for what God has and is still teaching me through it all.

Mark McDowell
October 21, 1955 ~ August 28, 1997

HOPE & HELPS

Scripture I clung to on the hardest days/nights:

- Psalm 37:4–7. Mark and I found out after we were engaged that this passage was precious to both of us as it had been an encouragement to each of us individually when we met. The key to this is not about getting what you want from God, but rather, delight in the Lord, commit your ways to Him, trust in Him, and rest in Him. His desires will become your desires.

- Jeremiah 29:11. I know this passage is for Israel, but as a child of God it is a reminder that God never intends evil for me.

Helpful things people did to minister to me:

- Just being aware. Checking on us. We had friends that would just show up after a heavy snow and plow the driveway or help cut up and haul off broken tree limbs.

- Letting us talk about Mark. Asking questions and listening. Helping keep his memory alive. Many people are uncomfortable with grief or just don't know what to say so they say nothing or change the subject.

What you should NOT say to someone in a similar circumstance:

- "I know how you feel." We truly do not know how someone else feels. We may be able to empathize more than someone else, but we do not know their feelings.

- "If you could see them now (in heaven), you would not wish them back here on earth." This makes the person suffering feel selfish because he or she does want them back. This does not offer comfort.

- "You need to consider remarriage. Your children need a father." Well, since God took their earthly father and He promises to be a father to the fatherless, then I trust Him to decide if that needs to happen.

Hymns or songs that comforted me:

- *It Is Well with My Soul,* Spafford/Bliss

- *His Way Is Perfect,* The Wilds

- Most hymns and praise music were and are a comfort. I kept music playing a lot. It is soothing and an encouragement.

The hope Jesus has given me through my loss of Mark:

- God is sovereign. I know He loves me. He never makes a mistake. He always does what is best. Those absolutes will not ever change. No matter how I may feel or what may be happening, those absolutes remain constant. I cannot trust my feelings or circumstances, but I can trust in God.

- I know I will see Mark in heaven again one day. Even though one of my biggest struggles was the reality that I will never be his wife again, we will enjoy sweet fellowship together and worship our Lord for all eternity.

WE SHALL WALK THROUGH THE VALLEY IN PEACE

A.L. Hatter

*The Lord your God is in your midst,
a victorious warrior.
He will rejoice over you with joy,
He will be quiet in His love,
He will rejoice over you with shouts of joy.*

Zephaniah 3:17

Soul

Emily Curtis

Oh soul, are you weighed down with sorrow,
Does grief seem your nearest kin?
Are you anxiously viewing tomorrow?
With a heart that is aching within?

Oh soul, do you feel the weight of this world,
As it moans under sin's dreaded curse?
Do you long for the day when He'll make all things new
Exchanging beauty for all that now hurts?

There is a day coming where all things will be
Beautiful, glorious, bright!
Where to eyes now darkened and filling with tears,
He will unveil His unfathomable light!

Oh, dear precious soul, remember the Truth,
That will not waiver nor wane,
That the Lord is your God, He will redeem all your days,
And what is lost here on earth will be Heaven to gain!

So ye, though you walk through the Shadowy Valley,
And your heart will be tempted to fear,
Remember, a shadow can only be cast
When the sun is drawing near.

Take courage, o soul, and cling to the Son,
When it seems only darkness surrounds.
Hold fast to His promises, finding them true
And you'll find it's His grace that abounds.

The Lord is good, a stronghold in the day of trouble;
He knows those who take refuge in Him.

Nahum 1:7

This Isn't Real

Chantell Dennis

I was sitting in my office mid-morning when my husband, Jared, walked into the building. My first thought was, is he surprising me with lunch? But then I saw his face. Something wasn't right. He walked into my office, shut the door, sat down, put his head in his hands and told me what he had just heard. He had just been laid off. His company went broke and laid off all of their employees on the same day with no warning.

"We'll figure this out; you'll get a new job; we'll be fine" were the words out of my mouth. And we were. God took care of us and He provided a job for Jared even better than the one he had before. He had a plan for Jared; He had a plan for us.

Jared was offered a position for a wonderful company with amazing benefits; it fit his qualifications perfectly. But first, he had to pass a health screening. No big deal, he was 25 and perfectly healthy. So, to the doctor he went. He passed his physical and just needed to complete a blood test.

Several hours later, Jared walked into my office again. This time, I knew something was really, truly wrong. He was crying. As he began to speak, my heart sank and in that moment I knew everything was going to change. This isn't real was the first thought that crossed my mind. He told me that the doctor had called him and told him something was wrong. His kidneys were barely working. In fact, they hadn't been for quite some time and the doctors were amazed that he was even functioning as he was. They needed him to come back in for some more testing to determine if this was a fluke.

Of course, this was a mistake. Jared was an all-star athlete; he was in great physical shape; he was young and active and healthy! This wasn't real. Hours later, the doctors called back again to confirm our worst fears. Jared's kidneys were only functioning at 10 percent and he was in need of a kidney transplant or he would have to go on dialysis.

This wasn't real. How could this be real? Where was God? Shouldn't He have prevented this? Shouldn't He have protected us from this? Why Jared? Why me? Why us? Questions I still don't have the answer to and I know I never will. One thing I do know, however, is that God was protecting Jared. If Jared had not been laid off of his job, we would not have found out about his kidney failure until it was far worse. Looking back, I see God's sovereignty in how and when He revealed this to us.

We prayed, we cried, we sought counsel, we asked for prayer, and in those first several months we felt very supported by our community. We felt prayed over and so many people got in line to see if they could be a match to donate a kidney to Jared. There were a few times when we got our hopes up that there was a match, only to be told that it didn't work out. Many months went by and it looked like Jared would have to go on dialysis soon. But we were both leaning on each other and trusting that the Lord had a plan.

In the midst of this trial, God brought us some joyous news—we were expecting our first child. A son! The day we were taking our baby announcement photos, I got a phone call from UCLA hospital. They had been doing the testing on Jared and potential donors and they had found a match. The donor has chosen to remain anonymous to this day, however, I can say that it was one of the last people I would have expected. This person didn't even tell us that he was getting tested; he was older, and his physique was so much smaller than my husband's. But God had created this person's kidney from the moment they were born, to be a match for Jared.

So many tears and prayers of rejoicing later, Jared received his kidney transplant. The donor recovered well and Jared's kidney was immediately accepted. The doctors were so excited to tell me that as soon as they hooked the kidney up, it began producing urine immediately. This was a great sign of a healthy kidney and a great match! We left the hospital a week later and everything seemed well.

We welcomed our first son in October and enjoyed two full years of health! God granted us so many blessings in those two years. I look back on that time with fondness, rejoicing in His care over us, His love, and His providence. God was good and He had been good to us. We prayed for a miracle and He answered!

However, things didn't stay that way for long. Jared began to get sick. It started with a lack of appetite, weight loss, a cough, and general lethargy. We had several weeks of wondering what was going on. We checked in with the doctors who thought he just had a cold. Jared was still functioning and working, and we even went to our friend's house to help them move. We had just finished helping them move a couch and were about to eat lunch when I looked at Jared and he didn't look well. He tried to speak, but his words came out jumbled and he passed out as I tried my best to catch him and lay him down. We went to the doctor later that day; they ran tests and told us they would call with the results.

The next day was Sunday. Jared was at work; I was at church when he called me. The doctors told him that his kidney had been rejected and he needed to check into the hospital immediately. I couldn't breathe. I couldn't think. I just thought, "This isn't real. This can't be real. We are happy; he was healthy; he is so young! This has to be a mistake." But it wasn't and the next six weeks, spent in the hospital, would be the worst six weeks of my life. I saw my strong husband, my rock, my everything, suffer in a way I never thought I would have to. No one knew what was happening or how to reverse it.

There were a lot of maybes, some improvement, and then some backsliding. The worst news was that there was now less than a 1 percent chance that Jared would find another match and be able to receive a second transplant. The future looked bleak. In the midst of all of this, I found out I was pregnant with our second child. It didn't seem possible to face this on my own. I was going back and forth between the hospital and home, trying to care for my one-year-old son, and be there with my husband. My heart was torn.

But God. He was with me every step of the way. Every drive to the hospital when I was crying out to Him to save my husband, every drive home when I was crying after watching him be poked and prodded and then having to leave him. And God was there every moment I spent with my son, when I was crying out to Him to save my husband so he could be a father to our children. There was no comfort like the one my God gave to me in those moments. A peace that surpassed all understanding. Knowing that in this moment God was perfecting me and my faith. He was going to use this for my good, and for my husband's good. Even though it didn't feel good.

Jared was able to come home after six weeks, but he would need to do dialysis three days a week. It was a horrible adjustment for him, and absolutely heart-breaking to watch him suffer through the headaches and side effects of this treatment. Jared was strong through it all.

Three days a week, he would go to the hospital to get his treatment from 4:00–7:00 am, then he would turn around and go to work. He would come home utterly exhausted and barely had the ability to do anything other than rest. For me, this was one of the loneliest times in my life. It felt as if the people that had been supporting us in the beginning, suddenly, didn't have much to say. It didn't seem as if they understood what we were going through and most of the time, it didn't seem that anyone cared to ask and find out.

Those two years were a complete blur and I now realize I was just functioning in survival mode during that time. I gave birth to our second son and found out we were pregnant with our daughter a year and a half later. They were good gifts, sweet additions to our family, but I felt as if I wouldn't be able to handle one more thing on my plate. During that time, I needed to be both mom and dad to our boys and still care for my husband. It was difficult, and I was exhausted, but God was my constant—my companion and my friend in those dark days.

He was growing me. He began to develop in me a true compassion for others. I am sad to say that before this trial, I was a critical person. I didn't have empathy for others and I lacked understanding of another's perspective. But going through this has taught me that everyone is going through something, and to give grace. Even though these days were difficult, I look back with thankfulness at how God chose to perfect our faith in this way. I see his kindness in gifting us with three children who brought laughter and true joy even on our darkest days.

Our story doesn't end there. Two years after being on dialysis, Jared received a phone call in the middle of the night from Mayo Clinic in Arizona. Someone currently on life support, who was an organ donor on the East Coast, was a match for Jared. It was a hard emotion to process. Grief for the family who was having to make a difficult decision and say goodbye to someone they loved, but at the same time, rejoicing that God had provided this second chance for Jared. The doctors had told us that there was less than a 1 percent chance that Jared would find a match.

But God.

We made it to Arizona the next day (with our two-month-old daughter) and Jared received his transplant. He was able to come home six weeks later and I have not taken one single day spent together as a family of five for granted. This trial has given me a thankfulness for life and for each moment with my husband. As I'm writing this, a year and a half later, there is always some worry about how long this current kidney is going to last. And that is something I will live with the rest of my life. But we are choosing to trust in the Lord and know that no matter what the circumstance, He will continue to provide.

Jared after his first
kidney transplant ∼ 2015

Jared and Chantell and kids:
Jack, Calvin, and Charlotte ∼ 2020

There was no comfort like the one my God gave to me in those moments. A peace that surpassed all understanding. Knowing that in this moment God was perfecting me and my faith. He was going to use this for my good, and for my husband's good. Even though it didn't feel good.

HOPE & HELPS

Scripture we clung to on the hardest days/nights:
Psalm 31; Psalm 91; Psalm 4:8; Psalm 139; Isaiah 26:3; Jeremiah 29:11

Helpful things people did to minister to us:
- Watched our kids
- Wrote notes
- Provided meals
- Visited in the hospital
- Sent gifts
- Continually reminded us that they were praying for us, and telling me (as the spouse) that they were praying for me.

What you should NOT say to someone in a similar circumstance:
- Compare your trials to his or hers.
- Say, "Let me know if you need anything." Instead, just do something!
- Make it about you.

Hymns or songs that comforted us:
- *Not for a Moment,* Meredith Andrews
- *Thy Will,* Hillary Scott

The hope Jesus has given us through our trial:
Every day is a gift and we shouldn't take it for granted. He has given me a hope for the next life and a longing for heaven, where there will be no more tears or suffering, where we will have new bodies, and we can be with Him forever.

I Surrender All

1. All to Je - sus I sur-ren-der, All to Him I free - ly give;
2. All to Je - sus I sur-ren-der, Make me, Sa - vior, whol - ly Thine;
3. All to Je - sus I sur-ren-der, Lord, I give my - self to Thee;

I will e - ver love and trust Him, In His pre-sence dai - ly live.
Let me feel Thy Ho - ly Spi - rit, Tru - ly know that Thou art mine.
Fill me with Thy love and po - wer, Let Thy bles-sing fall on me.

I sur-ren-der all, I sur-ren-der all;
I sur-ren-der all, I sur-ren-der all;

All to Thee, my bless - ed Sav - ior I sur-ren - der all.

Judson W. Van DeVenter

Winfield S. Weeden

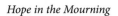

You will keep him in perfect peace,
whose mind is stayed on You,
because he trusts in You.

———

Isaiah 26:3 (ESV)

Surrender

Emily Curtis

Anxious thoughts swell within
My worn and weary soul.
Forlorn, forgotten and dismayed,
Left to suffer all alone.

Oh God, where is your comfort
As my cheeks are drenched in tears,
Where is the solace for my heart,
To quiet all my fears?

Hear my longing pleas
As I stammer in the night,
With groaning, Spirit, intercede;
Have mercy on my plight.

Then softly laid upon my mind,
He patiently replied:
"Surrender your worries, Precious One,
And I will lift you high."

"I'll place your feet upon high ground,
And plant you firmly there,
No longer will your trial surround,
Nor shall your heart despair."

The Lord God is my strength, and He has made my feet like hinds' feet,
and makes me walk on my high places.

Habakkuk 3:19

In His Holed Hands

Carrie J. Malik

"I just don't think I can be pregnant anymore."

I said this through the phone to my mother while driving to my final OB appointment and ultrasound. One last look to see the baby's position before the delivery date just twelve days away. I was tired. Nearing the end of my fourth pregnancy, with my fourth and final C-section already planned, I was just weary. My husband followed in the truck behind me with our three kids, one sick. He had been asked to be in another state that day for work, and I had begged him to stay nearby for no particularly good reason. "Just in case," I said. I'd never gone into labor in the past, but I was big, heavy, uncomfortable—and weary.

He waited in the parking lot with the kids. I sat in the waiting room and took a photo from above my full belly. "About to see baby via ultrasound and confirm (for the 5th time) that there's only one in there," I captioned. A stranger had recently, rudely, insisted that there "had to be more than one in there" more than once, and then uttered her final declaration that, "Well then, it must be one, huge baby!"

Cresha, the ultrasound tech who had scanned all of my babies, called me back to the room. We talked quietly and pleasantly, having known each other over the years, while she scanned. She made a few comments about the baby and printed me some photos. "I just want to step out real quick and get Dr. Shah."

I don't remember feeling particularly alarmed. I easily brushed off the thought, "That was weird, she didn't let me hear the heartbeat … probably because I'm so far along."

The doctor walked in and stopped. I was sitting with the photos in my lap that I had already sent by text to my husband, still waiting. I smiled at him. "Carrie, when did you last feel the baby move? She can't find the baby's heartbeat."

His words cut me to the marrow. "What? I don't know … ." The next moments are muddy. Hard to think clearly through. I called my husband and they brought him in and ushered our kids to a separate room. He asked, "Can you check again? Please? Are you sure?" I remember my eyes closed as I took in the sound of the silence of my womb. The quiet static of a heartbeat absent. One of us asked, "Can you please tell us if it's a boy or a girl, so we can name the baby?" We had looked forward to that surprise. "It's a girl. The baby's a girl."

With the details finalized for my delivery to be now later that evening, we headed out of the office with our kids. They asked questions that I don't recall as my husband, Basam, ushered them gently to the truck. We told them there in the parking lot that the baby had died, and that they had a sister. We all cried and our mourning as a family began. I silently prayed, depending heavily upon "the groaning" of our Comforter, the Holy Spirit, and stared out the window on the way home.

Basam talked and cried with his boss, "Let me just tell you what's needed so I can put it to rest." Dads, and their ever-present need to take care of all the things. Other texts and calls were made. Friends dropped everything to pray for us, help us, make calls. Our parents immediately traveled hundreds of miles to be with us and our children—to help with whatever was needed. A dear friend of Basam's drove to our home. I found him standing on the porch crying. "I just came," he told my husband in an embrace of earned brotherhood. "I just came. I didn't know what else to do."

A flurry of activity. Talking with the OB department, trying to anticipate our needs ... what was allowed? How much time would we have with her? Would our children be able to see her? We simply didn't know how to navigate waters we had never seen, in a boat without sails. No wind. On the phone with the photographer, a volunteer with Now I Lay Me Down to Sleep (remembrance photography for parents suffering the loss of a baby), packing things she suggested to make the first, last, and only photos we would ever have with our daughter. Talking with our beloved pastor, confirming and grateful for the peace of knowing that he would be with us that evening at the hospital to commend her to Him who holds. To pray with us who mourn. To remind our eyes to seek Him and His glory. Of all the happenings that afternoon, most vivid are the moments I exchanged loving, hurting glances with my husband, the tender ways he held me and our children, praying together on our bed, and our family discussion, determining her name. Precious name spoken to her by our Father in heaven, her Master Creator, the One she opened her eyes to hours before.

Gloria Micah.

Gloria. Offhandedly suggested by a friend, never formally written on "The Names List." But now? Was there any other name to give her? Impossible. Gloria. Because Gloria in Excelsis Deo, because to Him be all glory and praise. Because He is our Light in the darkness, because it carried the same melodic lilt and musicality, the same tender sounds as her older sister's name, Aria.

Micah. Beloved and missed son of a friend who understood our pain that day. Micah, proclaiming prophet, a fighter for justice, a pointer to our coming Messiah, confident in our Savior to come. "Therefore I will look to the Lord; I will wait for the God of my salvation; my God will hear me" (Micah 7:7).

Gloria Micah.

We drove to the hospital, seeing sun rays streaming down through a heavily cloudy day. We arrived, and my mom remembers me saying, "If I don't go in then it won't be real." We entered and checked in. Our hospital, where I also worked (and still do) as a nurse, wore like a favorite sweater. It was easier, I think, walking into a place where at least the lights, smells, sounds, and people weren't a barrage of unknowns. Most faces were familiar. A marker put on the door to my room, signaling to the staff who would enter, that we were grieving the death of our baby that day. The compassionate nurse prepping me for surgery started with a hug, and, "I'm so sorry this is your day." I had never been able, in four pregnancies, to labor and deliver; I had always required cesarean. I was thankful to be able to move into that familiar territory.

As I was on the operating table, Basam rubbed my arm—a tactile distraction from the tugging and pulling from below, all of it seeming to wrench my heart's strings. Thoughts ran through my mind: when she came out her lungs wouldn't fill; I would hear no first cry; and I would be left with the weighted, buried-in-sand sensation of numbness from surgery. Quickly, she was here. On the evening of October 15, 2014—the very day set aside by our nation to remember every baby lost during pregnancy, in stillbirth, or infancy—our Gloria entered the room. She was 6-pounds-13-ounces, of perfect, newborn-girl beauty. Skin like silk, hair like down, lips like delicate petals of a wine-red rose. We exclaimed over her as I cherished the welcome weight of her little frame on my chest. I kissed her. They placed her in her daddy's arms. Gloria's daddy. Born Muslim. Gloria's daddy, who had married me, professing Christian. This man of my heart who had spent years searching, seeking wise counsel from friends and pastors, trying to "logic" his way through faith in attempts to make sense of Jesus Christ and the truth of who He is. He later wrote, remembering his awakening:

"The moment they laid her—still—in my arms in the operating room, I knew I was at the bottom. I was so broken. Psalm 116:6 says, "When I was brought low, He saved me." It was at this moment, when there was nothing that I could do to save Gloria, that I prayed to the Lord. I felt the Holy Spirit. I felt His peace. He was there, assuring me that in Him, Jesus Christ, we are saved. He saves us all. Our life is eternal in Him. There was nothing I could do, there was only what Jesus had already done. It wasn't logic. It didn't make sense. It wasn't my "decision." At that moment, all of my questions were answered; all doubts removed; all chains of bondage released. I saw myself, just as helpless and lifeless as my daughter, as she lay in my arms! Yet, He reached down, lifted me up and gave me His peace. I knew that all of this was God's plan. Maybe it was her gift to me—to save someone—to be used to bring me to saving knowledge of Jesus Christ. Maybe that was God's plan for her life. She wasn't enough, and I didn't have to be enough. But Christ. Christ was enough. Christ IS enough. Christ will always BE enough."

My swollen belly closed, we were moved to recovery, our swaddled, silent daughter wrapped up with us. They ushered Pastor Dickie in to be with us privately. From his first meeting with Basam, this man had lovingly challenged my husband—always—to seek the God he had known since the days of his youth, starting in a locker room. Always pointing us to Christ. This man, one of the first to whom Basam would publicly proclaim his changed heart, his new love for Jesus; this man, who would eventually walk all of us into the waters of baptism, lifting us up, renewed before our church; he came for us, even before we "officially" belonged to his flock. Like Jesus, he left the 99 for the needs of one family that evening (Matthew 18:12). He gently lauded her beauty, wept and prayed for, with, and over us. His presence and voice, his calm assurance—welcomed gifts of steady peace in the swirling of the day.

I was moved into my room. Our children were there, visibly pained meeting their sister this way. They asked questions. They admired her. They held her, touching her fingers and toes and kissing her head. They held on to us. Grandparents held her, cried for this meeting—the first, the last, the everything, of their granddaughter. Brother sobbed, shaken. Pastor prayed, reminding us that heaven is a place for us to look forward to with great anticipation, and now, because someone we loved so very much was waiting for us, it was sweeter even still. He assured us all, "Let not your heart be troubled; you believe in God, believe also in Me. In my Father's house are many mansions; if it were not so, I would have told you. I go to prepare a place for you" (John 14:2). He spoke God's dependable truth, "There shall be no more death, nor sorrow, nor crying. There shall be no more pain" (Revelation 21:4). Kristy, our Now I Lay Me Down to Sleep photographer, was also there, her quiet angel wings of artful eye and soft exposure, photographing our moments. She helped our children choose clothes to dress Gloria. She helped position her in their arms. In Daddy's arms. In my arms. Helped us show our love and adoring of this terribly loved and desperately wanted daughter and sister. She prayed and wept quietly with us. What a gift to us, to secure forever, these moments with Gloria. The first, the last, the only moments. Every second a treasure to behold.

Our parents took our children home and helped settle them in for the night. Basam and I settled into the quiet. We were allowed to sleep with her. Hold her constantly. I didn't want too much medication, desiring to remember all of it no matter how hard or painful. The rest of our time at the hospital is murky for me. Hard to order its time and space. I remember messaging the entire world the next morning. I was desperate never to run into someone who hadn't seen, didn't know, and would inevitably ask, "How's the baby?" I remember the few visitors, tentative friends and coworkers, with their kind words and warm hugs.

I remember the frustration of wiping away the constant watery trickle from her mouth and nose, from lungs never having been cleared by breath and cry. I remember the first night, hearing the sounds of other babies crying and parents' hushed talking through the walls—it seemed comforting. Then the second night, those same sounds tortured me and made me want to scream. During one short time that I spent alone, I pressed one ear to the bed and the pillow to the other, trying to block out the sounds of the living.

I remember the look on the nurse's face when she told me the funeral home had arrived, and I asked, sobbing, "Is this the hardest part, when they take her away and I never hold her again?" She said yes, quiet and kind, standing beside me, thankfully present. I remember the humble funeral home director, who honored my motherly request, begging that she not be wrapped in a plastic shroud as my husband handed her to him. Wrapping her in white linen, he carried her away. I remember friends who arrived on the day of our leaving, to help usher us out to our car, arms empty and hearts full of mess. The feel of their love and the sound of our laughter helping ease the torment of empty arms. I remember my husband's hand on me constantly, holding me, helping me, and a constant reminder of our Father in heaven who held us all in His.

The next days were busy and full of preparations for burial and memorial. We didn't know how else to "do" this thing called grief and death, so we just hit it head-on and embraced the fullness of it all. We tried to be open. Welcoming those who were grieving alongside and for us. At the church, we heard treasured scripture, lifted voice to songs both new and old, blanketing our heart with His truth. The praises of the mourning rose. We spoke to all gathered there, together, as husband and wife, of her short life with us. Of our thankfulness for the outpouring of love and support. Of our good and perfect God who had provided for us, thus far, in more ways than we could put to proper word. Friends, family, and church body brought gifts in plenty, food to feed us, their company, their cards, and their continued prayers.

We settled in. Settled in to the grief, slowly moving back toward what we thought was normal. But life AG, "after Gloria," had just started. We tend to measure it that way now, BG and AG, "before Gloria" and "after Gloria." Slowly at first, then all of a sudden, it began to feel unraveling. Everything was hard. At home, hurting kids hurt each other. Hurting parents hurt kids. Hurting spouses hurt one another. I said to a friend, "It's like it's all falling apart." I would write long lists of thanks, mostly for myself, a forced praise of "Thank you, God, for this day" that required my constant search for goodness. Then there were days when my groanings and tears could form no words but would shake my body and choke hard on my throat. We moved through days, weeks, months, still grieving, because it isn't something that you ever get over. I wrote in December 2015, "Grief isn't whatever stomach ailment is going around. We still grieve because grief is something that you carry. We grieve what cannot be fixed. We simply learn how to survive with it. How to carry it with us. We are forever changed since Gloria's death."

We sought guidance and support, and realized our need to surround ourselves with people who understood. The Lord led us to a center for grieving families. There, in our own groups, through conversation, group activities, music, art, and other planned activities, we learned to embrace what loving her looked like. There we learned it was okay to just not be okay some days. There we learned that support and understanding means something. That no one can truly understand because it was our loss. Our story. Our road to walk.

Through the grace of God, He began the slow healing of our hearts. Of tendering us to the goodness and sovereignty of His plan for our family. It has now been six years since she was born into the arms of Jesus. Six years of trusting His plan. Six years of bending the desires of our hearts to His will. Six years of celebrating the moments we had with her, and treasuring that she is ours. Six years of looking forward with hope for the time we will have together in eternity, where all of this hurt and hardness will be healed— our hearts whole, in Him. Last year, for her fifth birthday, I wrote again for her.

She'd Be a Whole Hand Today

She'd be a whole hand today. One two three four five little fingers tasting the sweetness, pulling the candles out of the cake one by one to lick the frosting.

She'd be a whole hand today. One two three four five little fingers pressing up, spread wide, saying "look Momma, I'm this many."

She'd be a whole hand today. One hand reaching up to touch my cheek because I hold her like a baby still, and sing.

She'd be a whole hand today. Five fingers squeezing around one or two of mine or Daddy's when we look both ways, or meander walking in the fading evening.

She'd be a whole hand today. Five fingers on each hand pressing my cheeks while she stares into my momma eyes with her baby-girl brown eyes, little loose curls on the underside of her hair at her nape.

She'd be a whole hand today. Writing her name slowing and scratching,
maybe she makes her G backward. Or forgets to dot her "i."
Tracing letters with her pointer as she learns her ABCs.

She'd be a whole hand today. Reaching up to hug her daddy tight, little arms
squeezing his neck. Saying "love you most and beyond, I win" because,
of course, her big sister would've taught her that line that's said many times
some days, racing to be the first to say it.

She'd be a whole hand today. Reaching out, doggy paddling,
"Help me swim, Daddy!" And flying, jumping into his wet arms, splashing.

She'd be a whole hand today. Rubbing his cheek and calling him scratchy,
squealing when his face whiskers tickle her as he smothers her with his kisses.

She'd be a whole hand today. Squeezing her brothers' hands
while they swing her up into the air, after counting one-two-three.

She'd be a whole hand today. Carrying too many books
and snuggling up next to the boys saying, "Read these to me pease."

She'd be a whole hand today. Hers clutching the steering wheel of the tractor,
filled with joy and riding through the yard in brother's lap.

She'd be a whole hand today. Wrapped around a too-big fishing pole,
with brother leaned in, helping hold, waiting for the bobber to sink.

She'd be a whole hand today. He'd teach her, help her, pull the wriggling worms
up out of the dirt, laugh when she squeals, helping her hold the backyard garters.

She'd be a whole hand today. Playing dolls with her big sister,
little fingers braiding her hair. Putting on lip gloss and sparkling eye shadows.

She'd be a whole hand today. Touching piano notes together,
our two girls on the bench, singing Jesus Loves Me sweetly.

She'd be a whole hand today. Snuggling under grandma quilts
and learning her numbers, as loving sister helps her hand
to hold the crochet hook, trace the picture, color the pages.

She'd be a whole hand today. Squeezing in to close our family circle when we pray.

A whole hand.

She's a whole hand today.

A whole hand of years spent in heaven.

A whole hand of years we've felt the weight of her absence.

Been without her.

Missed. Every. Little. Thing.

A whole hand.

Gloria, her whole hands, rest in His holed hands. Maybe she holds onto Him, sits at His feet—the Savior and Father she opened her bright, quiet eyes to on the morning that she left us. Maybe she raises her healed hand to shield her face while basking in His glory.

She is wholly healed, and wholly His.

Wholly His. She rests in His hands. His holed hands. The hands He showed the disciples when He said, "See My hands and My feet, that it is I Myself; touch Me and see" (Luke 24:39). His holed hands. The evidence of His finished work, done for us, through His death and resurrection. She rests in His hands, the same way that our three living children do. We work to make them ours, we wrestle in our ownership of them as our children. But ultimately, they're His. His to work in. His to will and to do for His good pleasure (Philippians 2:13). So, we rest. We anticipate our future, together in Christ. We cling tightly to "this hope we have as an anchor of the soul, both sure and steadfast" (Hebrews 6:19). This hope is Him, our Lord and Savior, Jesus Christ. And by His grace, and in His holed hands, we rest.

Gloria's siblings meeting her

Basam & Carrie comforting one another with Gloria

Gloria Micah Malik
October 15, 2014

HOPE & HELPS

Scripture we clung to on the hardest days/nights:
Jeremiah 1:5; Micah 7:7; Lamentations 3:22–26; Psalm 139, especially an adaptation, written from God's point of view.

Helpful things people did to minister to us:
- Delivered meals. Recovering from surgery as well as the loss of a child, this was a welcome gift for my family of five.

- Gifts. Especially things with her initials or her name.

- Sending flowers or cards for future birthdays.

- Simple text messages or calls or notes telling us that she was thought of for some particular reason, especially as months and years pass.

- Saying her name. Vague references are dismissive and sometimes hurtful. Say her name. You cannot remind us that our child died. We can never forget!

- Remember the dads. They lost a child too, and so much focus is on the momma.

- Remember the siblings. Their sister died.

What you should NOT say to someone in a similar circumstance:
- "Do you think she was in pain when the cord was wrapping around her neck?" If I hadn't thought of this, do you actually want me to think about this? Stop, and think really hard before you ask questions that no one can answer. Better yet, don't ask the bereaved at all.

- "Oh honey, it's okay, you're young and can have more babies; it'll be fine." Do you know that? Are you sure? Because I wasn't young in maternal years, and we didn't have more babies. It's not fine. I can rest in the sovereignty of God, absolutely, but I wanted her. I wanted that baby, not to put a replacement on order. Regardless of the number of children, the weeks into the pregnancy, the age of the child, the parent wanted that child—alive.

- Basam's least favorite is, "At least you have other kids." We wanted this one too. My other children, while I'm thankful for them, don't replace my dead child.

- Platitudes, too many to repeat. But the top two are:
  o "God won't give you more than you can handle." This is unbiblical and a complete lie. I'm probably guilty of using it, or even agreeing with it. However, He gives us more than we can handle, on a regular basis, so that we can rely on Him and His strength. So that He can be our strength, our power. Amen.
  o "You must really be strong for God to know you could get through this." That makes this seem like a punishment. Because I am strong, He chose to take my child to heaven? It's also unbiblical. I am weak. I am a mess without Jesus. "And He said to me, 'My grace is sufficient for you, for My strength is made perfect

in weakness.' Therefore most gladly I will rather boast in my infirmities, that the power of Christ may rest upon me" (2 Corinthians 12:9).

Hymns or songs that comforted us:
- Her name is Gloria. So, any song that sings her name, especially *Angels We Have Heard on High,* The Piano Guys version, is our favorite. We play this Christmas song any time we feel like it!
- *It Is Well with My Soul,* Spafford/Bliss
- *Amazing Grace,* John Newton
- *Ten Thousand Reasons,* Matt Redman
- *My Hope Is in You,* Aaron Schust
- *Blessings,* Laura Story
- *The Broken Beautiful,* Ellie Holcomb
- *I Will Carry You,* Selah
- *Gone Too Soon,* Daughtry

The hope that Jesus has given us through our loss of Gloria:
The hope of eternity together as a family, with Him. Heaven is that much sweeter to us because our daughter waits for us there. No matter how broken we are, in Him we are made whole.

I didn't have to be enough.
But Christ.
Christ was enough. Christ IS enough.
Christ will always BE enough.

How Can I Keep from Singing

My life flows on in end-less song;_ a-bove earth's la - men-
Through all the tu - mult and the strife, I hear the mu - sic
What though my joys and com-forts die?__ The Lord my Sa - vior
The peace of Christ makes fresh my heart, a foun-tain e - ver

ta - tion,_____ I catch the sweet, though far off hymn_ that
ring - ing,_____ It finds an ech - o in my soul._ How
liv - eth._____ What though the dark - ness gath - er round? Songs
spring ing!_____ All things are mine since I am His!_ How

hails a new cre - a- tion._ No storm can shake my in-most calm_ while
can I keep from sing ing?_
in the night he giv eth._
can I keep from sing ing?_

to that Rock I'm cling- ing_____ Since Christ is Lord of_____

hea-ven and earth, how can I keep_____ from sing ing?_____

Robert Low'ry

*A*nd He has said to me,
   "My grace is sufficient for you,
   for power is perfected in weakness."
Most gladly, therefore, I will rather boast about my weaknesses,
   so that the power of Christ may dwell in me.
Therefore I delight in weaknesses, in insults, in distresses,
   in persecutions, in difficulties, in behalf of Christ;
   for when I am weak, then I am strong.

2 Corinthians 12:9–10

My Darling Child

Emily Curtis

O Little eyes what did you see,
When your very first gaze was on pure glory?

O Little nose did you smell the sweet
Aroma of flowers near Jesus' feet?

Did you wrap your tiny, silky, soft hand,
Round that of the One who created water and land?

Did your perfectly formed ears hear the sound
Of angels singing praise to the Lamb all around?

Did you taste of the River of Life, Little One?
Did you breathe in the beauty of the Celestial sun?

How my heart yearns for that day,
When I'll see you again and He'll wipe tears away.

Until then, my darling, I'll cherish you dearly,
Anticipating the moment when I'll gather you near me.

Do not let your heart be troubled; believe in God, believe also in Me.
In My Father's house are many rooms; if that were not so,
I would have told you, because I am going there to prepare a place for you.
And if I go and prepare a place for you, I am coming again
and will take you to Myself, so that where I am, there you also will be.
And you know the way where I am going.

John 14:1–4

Anchored

Denise Edmond

This hope we have as an anchor of the soul, a hope both sure and steadfast.
—Hebrews 6:19

———

*"If the storms don't cease, and if the winds keep on blowing,
my soul has been anchored in the Lord."* —Douglas Miller

"Anchor" means to fix or rest on. Keep this in mind.

In this thing called life, storms are imminent. It's always a good idea to be anchored before the storm comes! My life for many years was spent studying the Word and in prayer. This, I had been taught, was a sure way to get anchored. As providence would have it, I would need an anchor sooner than I thought.

One morning, while getting dressed for the day, a thought occurred to me: you and your family have not experienced hard times lately. It's been blessing upon blessings of late. Just about two years before, my husband had taught our family through the book of Job. In Job, we see the suffering of a man—a righteous man according to the Lord but, more importantly, we see the sovereignty of God.

Little did I know what was on the horizon. In the days, weeks, and months ahead, the Anchor (who is Jesus Christ) is just what I needed to steady me, to keep me from going overboard.

In March 2018, my brother died. Then, five days later a close family friend died (she was also my mother's best friend and our Bible study teacher). In another five days, my 99-year-old mother died. Would you say I needed an Anchor? Would you have needed an Anchor?

My husband gave my mom's eulogy and, once we buried her, I thought the storm was over. Instead, due to some things happening with my husband's body (we thought it might be work related), a doctor's appointment became necessary. I went to the doctor with him but not in the exam room. When he came out, I could see on his face that the news was concerning. I asked, "What did he say?" He said, "I have cancer."

That is one diagnosis no one wants to hear. All I could think to say in those moments was, "We'll fight this; I'm with you all the way." Oh, and Lord have mercy! You see, He is my Anchor! He alone knows how to fix me to rest on Him.

Scans were scheduled, which led to the first surgery. We still did not know just how dire the situation or the stage of the cancer. All we wanted was to get it out of his body. After surgery, we were told that it had reached the lymph nodes. After working in the medical field for years, I knew that reaching the lymph nodes was not good.

Chemotherapy was our next move. Before chemotherapy could get started, we had to get out of the hospital. The night after surgery my husband began vomiting like you would not believe. I didn't believe it and I was there. Lord, what is going on? His nurse went to work contacting the doctors on-call, trying to get a plan. It took a good portion of the night and into the morning with him going on vomiting for what seemed to be an eternity.

As morning began to break, we were told that he had a bowel obstruction. His only relief was to put a gastrostomy tube (G-tube) down his nose. As you would expect, the process was harder on him than me, but you couldn't tell that by the prayers and tears I prayed and shed. On the second try, finally it was in, working to give him relief. Honestly, recalling this, I am more sure than ever that "the Anchor holds though the ship is battered, though the sails are torn; the Anchor holds in spite of the storm (Douglas Miller)."

After several days, the doctor ordered the removal of the G-tube. It appeared to have worked. But as soon as it was removed the vomiting resumed. So, the process was repeated, getting the tube down (this time on the first try, thank God), and me crying and praying. We were still leaning into Jesus, resting in our Anchor.

After scans, the doctors determined that another surgery was needed to correct things. So, they go back into the same incision and correct the problem. My husband comes back to the hospital room with no pain, just thankfulness that it's behind him. It's still a couple of days before the tube is removed and we are discharged from the hospital.

I will never forget, when we arrived home, it was a bright sunshiny day; my husband got out of the car and I went inside the house with our luggage. I went back to the door to see where he was and discovered him standing outside, looking up toward heaven intently. Thanking God, I suspect. It was for sure a day of thankfulness! The storm seemed to be behind us.

Moving forward, more scans (to make sure the cancer hadn't spread) and port-a-cath placement so that chemotherapy could begin. All seemed to be going well, only some hair loss and a day or two of exhaustion. His appetite was good, spirits up. Yes, we were on the upside of this. No need to involve the children and other family members when things seemed to be going so well. Being just three treatments away from ringing the bell, (ringing the bell is a tradition in cancer centers when treatments have been completed), he developed low back pain and a fever. They had told us fevers of 101 needed to be reported. They were running right at 100.

I stepped out for about two-and-a-half hours on a Saturday morning and when I got back, he was gone. I called and he said that we would talk when he got home; he was at urgent care. He was given an antibiotic. Antibiotics are good … when they work. This one did not!

For several days a fever ensued. The day of chemotherapy we saw the doctor first. Because of the fevers, we could not have the treatment but instead were sent straight to the hospital. By the time we reached the car, the prayers and tears could not be contained. It took a minute to get ourselves together. We traveled to the hospital in silence. I cannot quote you a verse of Scripture or lyrics to a song that would explain how we made it through this second storm. All I know is, He alone knows how to fix us to rest on Him!

The number of days we spent in the hospital was more than I cared to count, but enough that they finally discharged him with a prognosis of six months, maybe a year, because the cancer he had was very aggressive. I (we) thought the chemotherapy was working, but found out the cancer seemed to be feeding on it. Two extended hospital stays, two discharges, and we were home again. But this time we needed a plan. We had to share this devastating news with our children. That was hard.

We had a follow-up appointment with his urologist, which ended up being yet another surgery. After the appointment, I reached out to our children with a day and time for them to meet at our house for dinner. Though they knew about the cancer, they didn't yet know the prognosis. My sister and her two children wanted to be there to support us. As I was settling the grandchildren, my husband shared the news and the fact that he had another surgery in a few days. We had hopes of a quick in-and-out of the hospital. The tears, emotions, suggestions of how we could move forward were all recognized. We all agreed to believe God for complete healing. It was an evening and night to say the least.

The third surgery was underway. The doctor had thought after recovery he could go home, however, after the surgery (because of a history of complications) he wanted to keep him overnight. The fever returned. To administer proper treatments of medications, a PICC (peripherally inserted central catheter) line was put in. I think every antibiotic known to man (and maybe some not known to man) was tried. We were transferred from the palace (a huge room in a small hospital) to the pit (a tiny room in a large hospital). A new doctor came in with news that we were going to be moved to ICU (intensive care unit), which was better-equipped to handle things should he stop breathing.

Wow, what in the world … we have six months. We were planning for him to retire and do some traveling. This could not be happening—but it was.

So, the upside of ICU was its size. We could all visit; the room was huge. Our children wanted to meet all his doctors to see what they could tell them; they needed answers. When the meeting ended, the doctors, along with our children, came in and told us that all they could do now is keep my husband comfortable.

He was moving to palliative care. He would not be going home. Palliative care gave us their largest room. They made a bed for me and put it next to him so that we could hold hands as we drifted off to sleep. Between ICU and palliative care, the visitors, cards, calls, and prayers were innumerable. Through it all, God was fixing us to rest on Him!

William never lost his presence of mind. He conducted business with our daughter and played Jeopardy all from his ICU bed. One early morning (about two o'clock) we, along with our daughter, sang praises to our great God, our Anchor.

William had taught Sunday School to a group of teen boys years earlier, and when they visited him, they would say, "See you later." His response was, "Make sure you do." He didn't want them to miss heaven!

Some things he said to me: "I love you so, so much. I wanted to take care of you for the rest of your life." He had done that for 44 years. "I didn't know it would be like this; He makes you ready to see Him." And, "I hate to leave y'all, but I'm ready to go. I want to see my Savior's face!"

After we told our children, my husband lived 12 days. It was quick! My husband transitioned on October 8, 2018. His last breath landed on my right cheek. At that point he was in the presence of the Lord. He was with his Savior. He was with his Anchor!

A favorite thought from a devotional was comforting: "This is not the end of the story, it's only a chapter." I heard a message at a funeral a year or two after William was gone and what was said has been of great help. Did I want William healed or did I want him HEALED? Did I want him to live or did I want him to LIVE?!

From *The Anchor Holds*, by Ray Boltz:

The Anchor holds though the ship is battered
The Anchor holds though the sails are torn
I have fallen on my knees as I face the raging seas
The Anchor holds in spite of the storm

As I turn the page and do life now without my husband, I want to share a little about him. My husband, William R. Edmond, Sr., was a man of character. By profession, he was a licensed aircraft mechanic. He was a tinkerer, so the grands nicknamed him "Bob the Builder," because if their Papa couldn't fix it, it couldn't be fixed. He taught himself how to build and work on computers (his side hustle). He was really smart! He shared household responsibilities; by that I mean he did them all. From paying bills, grocery shopping, cooking (and he could outcook me any day of the week), and cleaning the kitchen. He spoiled me.

I love and miss him so much but he fought a good fight; he finished his course; he kept the faith. He's with Jesus and one day I will be too! My hope has found a resting place and it is in the Lord Jesus Christ. What about you? Have you placed your hope and faith in Him? He never disappoints! Thank you for taking time to read this chapter in my book of life.

William and Denise Edmond
2003

William R. Edmond, Sr.
August 6, 1956 ~ October 8, 2018

HOPE & HELPS

Scripture I clung to on the hardest days/nights:
Proverbs 3:5–6; Proverbs 18:10; 1 Samuel 7:12b

Helpful things people did to minister to me:
- Calls
- Prayers
- Sharing scriptures
- Meals
- Gift cards

What you should NOT say to someone in a similar circumstance:
- "He's already healed!"

Hymns or songs that comforted me:
- *He Will Hold Me Fast,* Keith and Kristyn Getty
- *My Heart Is Filled with Thankfulness,* Keith and Kristyn Getty

The hope that Jesus has given me through my loss of William:
- That He will take care of me.
- That I can rest in His Love for me.

He finished his course;
he kept the faith.
He's with Jesus and one day
I will be too!

ABIDE WITH ME

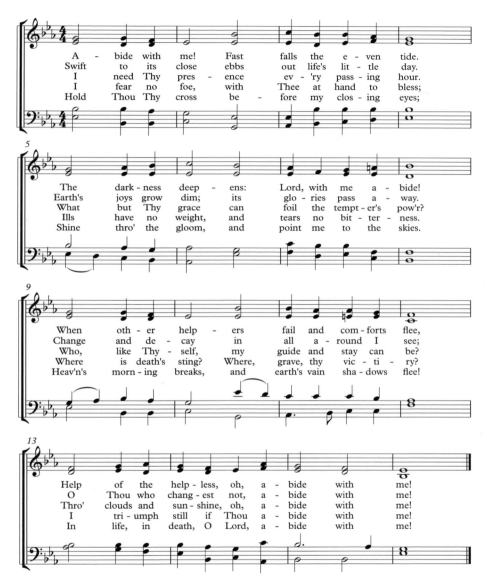

A - bide with me! Fast falls the e - ven tide.
Swift to its close ebbs out life's lit - tle day.
I need Thy pres - ence ev - 'ry pass - ing hour.
I fear no foe, with Thee at hand to bless;
Hold Thou Thy cross be - fore my clos - ing eyes;

The dark - ness deep - ens: Lord, with me a - bide!
Earth's joys grow dim; its glo - ries pass a - way.
What but Thy grace can foil the tempt - er's pow'r?
Ills have no weight, and tears no bit - ter - ness.
Shine thro' the gloom, and point me to the skies.

When oth - er help - ers fail and com - forts flee,
Change and de - cay in all a - round I see;
Who, like Thy - self, my guide and stay can be?
Where is death's sting? Where, grave, thy vic - ti - ry?
Heav'n's morn - ing breaks, and earth's vain sha - dows flee!

Help of the help - less, oh, a - bide with me!
O Thou who chang - est not, a - bide with me!
Thro' clouds and sun - shine, oh, a - bide with me!
I tri - umph still if Thou a - bide with me!
In life, in death, O Lord, a - bide with me!

Words: Henry F. Lyte   ©MichaelKravchuk.com   William H. Monk

*T*rust in the Lord with all your heart,
and lean not on your own understanding;
in all your ways acknowledge Him,
and He will make your paths straight.

Proverbs 3:5–6

Be Still

Emily Curtis

The very God who we cry out to when our hearts are heavy
and full of anguish is, Himself, acquainted with our grief;
He bore our suffering and He is not removed from our sorrows.

Beloved, rest your weary head upon His breast
and He will give you peace that passes your comprehension.
He will shelter you under His wings
and He will exchange your yoke for His.

When you call upon His name in the valleys,
behold He is there and He bends down to listen.
If it is He that you seek and in His name your hope is placed,
you shall not be disappointed.
Never shall He leave you nor shall He forsake you.

His plans for you are kind and altogether good.
Though the valley be dark and mountain steep,
fear not, He is working all things together for your good.
In your weakness, He shall sustain you with His unfathomable strength.
There is none on earth nor in Heaven like our God.

There is not one created thing that can thwart the mighty hand of the Creator.
The very waves obey His voice and with a word are stilled.
The Heavens declare His glory and not a sparrow falls without His watchful eye.

Take courage, precious one,
for far more dear to Him are you than any other created thing.
Take courage and find your rest in Him
for He will fight for you, you need only be still.

Have I not commanded you? Be strong and courageous! Do not be terrified
nor dismayed, for the Lord your God is with you wherever you go.

Joshua 1:9

His Name Is Love

Zoe Jones

There was never a day I questioned whether or not I was a Christian. Of course I was, after all, I believed in God. I believed the Bible was true, I believed in heaven and hell, and knew I wasn't going to hell … oh, yes, I was. Had the Lord chosen to take my life just before I turned 50, I was doomed and destined for hell for eternity. I know that now but didn't know that then.

I grew up in a Christian home with several pastors in my family. I came from a strong lineage of Christians. My grandfather, his father, and my uncle were all preachers. Of course, I was a Christian. I guess I believed somehow by osmosis, due to my rich Christian heritage and believing in God, I was a Christian. I prayed the prayer every year at camp. I walked the aisle a few times, was baptized, did the things that I was "supposed" to do, but I absolutely missed the message of salvation. Which is to repent and literally turn from sin and follow Christ.

I attended great churches all my life, churches that preached the gospel, but I was blind and deaf and actually pretty dumb. I used to joke when trying to have a spiritual conversation with someone that "I must have been absent that week" since I had no idea what they were talking about. I set out to read the Bible many times but never really understood what I read. I never repented and surrendered my life to Christ. Ever. I never died to self. But I didn't know that.

Grown, with a husband and children, we attended church, served, listened to Christian music, and cried with emotion listening to the words. I prayed and pled with God to "protect our family" and give us this or give us that. We had our children in Sunday school and Awana—until it got in the way of worldly things. "But be doers of the word, and not hearers only, deceiving yourselves" (James 1:22). I was a hearer only. I allowed sin and selfishness to completely rule my life. I guess I though God was a genie in a bottle or something! Deception!

When baseball practice or other things became more important than church, we sacrificed church. When all the worldly things became the focus because Christ really wasn't, weekly church attendance dropped. There was baseball practice or karate on Wednesday nights, so Awana was out. We were fueled by worldly things and not things that truly mattered. Our example to our children about Christ was that it had to be convenient, not a sacrifice.

Fast forward to a life of making other things more important than godly things. I was so caught up in it I was snowballing in sin, selfishness, and pride. I was discontent with most things in my life, so I found other things to fill the holes. Newsflash: you can't fill empty holes without Christ. Nothing satisfies like Christ.

I was constantly unsatisfied. I was discontent. I wanted more. After 21 years of marriage, I chose to leave. There was no biblical reason for divorce. I was simply done. Our children were struggling in the teen years; we didn't see eye to eye regarding discipline. My husband "didn't support me" with my passions; I didn't respect him. The economic downturn hit us hard and counseling wasn't helping.

I moved our daughter with me to Arizona where I had family, while our son was entering his first year of college in another state. The divorce caused our son great trauma through his college years. Pretty selfish, huh? Yep! Even as I drove away from our home with my husband standing in the middle of street, I knew I was doing the wrong thing. We lived in a darling neighborhood with one entrance/exit and it wrapped around in a circle with cute little houses. As I drove away in a U-Haul, I looked in the rearview mirror and wanted to wrap around the circle to go back. But I didn't. My pride was too strong. I had to go. Afterall, I said this is what I wanted and, by gosh, I was going to have what I wanted. I told myself all the lies I needed to justify my leaving.

After moving to Arizona, I got a great job, an apartment, and kept telling myself I had done the right thing. He didn't love me the way I wanted to be loved; he didn't provide well enough; he wasn't nice enough; he wasn't blah, blah, blah.

All the while, setting up my new life, I knew I was doing wrong. I couldn't even find happiness now. Maybe I'd be happy after the divorce was final. Maybe that would do it. But remember, I thought I was a Christian. There was no infidelity or physical abuse. I needed to find another "biblical" reason for divorce so God would honor it and I would feel justified. As Satan would have it, a few months after moving, while visiting our son in California, I went in a local bookstore looking for a book that would give me an out in my marriage. I went directly to the Christian book section.

As I looked at titles, I noticed a man hovering in the same isle. He must have sensed I wasn't finding what I was looking for. Turns out he was actually a local pastor of a well-attended church (that we actually attended but he didn't know that) and said he "made it a point to help people search for what they were looking for." I explained that I was looking for a book on Christian divorce. He said, "You won't find it here, but you can go online and get it," and gave me the name of a book and the author. (The author of the book now renounces his position and denounces divorce). The pastor told me that if I ever told anyone who recommended the book to me, he'd deny it. And actually has to this day. It's not his fault I sought divorce. It was totally mine. However, the book he recommended gave me exactly what I was looking for—a rationalization for divorce! I could biblically divorce essentially because my husband didn't meet my emotional needs. I filed for divorce right away and never looked back.

There were a few people that confronted me, but I blew them off. I had no interest in listening to anyone that wanted to help me see my sin. People offered to counsel us, talk with us, mediate for us—but I was out; I had what I was looking for and that was it!

As you would guess, the Lord had other plans for my life—my life without Him. I was fraught with disappointment, pain, and sadness. My conscious knew I had done the wrong thing, but I was good at getting my way. I was good at sinning and somehow thinking that I was a Christian. Somehow, I thought God would forgive me and that my life would be full. I spent years searching for happiness, the right job, the right man (a story in itself), all the things I wanted and thought I needed, but what I ended up with was endless days and years of heartache and discontentment.

But God.

Job 42:2 says, "No purpose of yours can be thwarted." God had a plan. He had a plan from before time began. He chose me. He chose to save me. On September 15, 2013, I learned what true repentance was and what a relationship with Jesus was supposed to look like. I was in church with my daughter. I can't remember what the pastor was preaching, but I looked at my daughter and said "I'm not a Christian." I don't even know if she heard me, but I sat there with the deepest feeling of sadness and disappointment I ever felt. I realized was not saved.

How was this possible? How was it that all my life I thought I was saved? I was self-deceived. Other people knew, how did I not know? I wasn't fooling anyone but myself for 50 years.

That was the most difficult realization of my life and yet the most important. Somehow, after all the years of church, crying out to God, and trying to read my bible, I missed the entire meaning of salvation: repenting and turning from my sin. I never surrendered my life to Christ. I was trying to control my life and let me tell you, it was out of control.

Again, I thought that because I believed there was a God and believed He would return one day, that I was saved. But I never lived for Him. I never longed for Him. I never died to self. I was never set apart from the world. Ever. Until that day, I had never been redeemed. Colossians 1:13–14 says, "He has delivered us from the domain of darkness and transferred us to the kingdom of his beloved Son in whom we have redemption, the forgives of sins." The veil was removed! I could see it all so clearly now. I had eyes to see my sin and selfishness and I had an incredible desire to know my savior, to turn from my sin, and to trust and follow Him with every part of my being.

I love Galatians 2:20: "I have been crucified with Christ. It is no longer I who live, but Christ who lives in me." Oh, God is so good. So good to reveal my sin to me so that I could finally turn and live for him. I was done "playing" Christian. I surrendered my life to Christ in a chair in my living room and longed to serve Him all the days of my life. I sat for hours and hours in that chair and repented of as many of my grievous sins as I could recall. I sat and cried and poured out my heart to God. I relived so many things that I wasn't sure I would ever be the same. Praise God, I was right, I was never the same again. So unworthy yet so thankful. I love that I had nothing to do with my salvation. I always tried to control everything! But I was always out of control. I had nothing to do with the redemptive work of the cross and what Christ did for me. I was fully His.

After God saved me and transformed my life, at 50 years old, knowledge of Scripture flooded back to me. Biblical truths I had heard all my life became something I understood, songs I remembered with words that had true meaning to me now. My entire world looked and sounded so different! I began to understand; I was finally born-again! I was able to read the Bible with understanding. I learned that my life was filled with idolatry, wants and desires that could never be met. It's funny, before I became a Christian, I thought idolatry was just worshipping religious or spiritual gods.

It never crossed my mind that an idol was anything I worshipped more than Christ. I had many idols I needed to put away.

As I grew in my early faith, by His grace alone, God allowed an opportunity for me to reach out to my ex-husband which is something we NEVER thought would happen. His sweet mother got breast cancer and I wanted him to know that I was praying. I wanted him to know that actually meant something now that I surrendered my life to Christ. We had a few texts back and forth regarding his mom, and then I was able to seek his forgiveness for destroying our marriage and family. Oh, what grace our Savior gives!

Robert was kind and tender and said that he had forgiven me years ago! What?! Wow, how could he? He said he had heard John MacArthur once say that "you are never more like Christ than when you can forgive." Oh, my heart was stirred. Would I have been able to offer that same grace and forgiveness? Could I forgive him if it was him that destroyed our marriage and children? At that moment I prayed that I would. I prayed for God to give me a spirit of forgiveness, chief of all sinners!

Robert and I began to talk more and more and share how God had transformed our lives over the years. We talked about areas in our lives where we failed one another and our failed our children. We sought forgiveness from one another where we disregarded each other. Text conversations began to be a daily thing. I was thankful to have connection with him again. I think I was about 12 when we met across the street from my aunt and uncle's house. He was my first junior high "boyfriend." We attended the same church; he cleaned our pool and was friends with my brother. We had a lifetime of history together. The connection was good.

Months went by and our daughter was going to visit her dad in California. She asked me to come and stay at a nearby hotel, and after she spent a few days with her dad we could hang out at the beach. The night before we left, she said she had talked with her dad and he said he wanted us both to stay with him. He would give up his room for us. Again, what?! Who does that? What kind of man would even want his sinner ex-wife near him, let alone sleep in our old bed!

I hadn't seen him in over five years! We pulled up to his house and he was standing outside waiting. Oh, my goodness, do I shake his hand, hug him, do nothing? I didn't know how to act. I got out of the car and he gave us both a hug and he took our suitcases upstairs. When I walked in his apartment I was shook. Our table, our chairs, our couch, our things. Then, I walked in the bedroom—our bed, our same sheets and comforter! I was shaking! How could he not get rid of everything that was ours! How did he not hate me?!

He took us to a nice dinner, and we walked around his little beach town and were friendly. Oddly it felt like we had seen each other recently. It felt nice, comfortable, normal. Later that evening, after our daughter fell asleep, we sat for hours—talking, seeking forgiveness, and shedding our brokenness to one another. The next night we did the same; we talked until the very wee hours of the morning. There wasn't enough time to say all we had to say. Just as we were getting ready to end the conversation, he asked a very bold question. He asked what I wanted, what did I want for my life. I took a few seconds to respond, then told him I wanted our old life back, but with Christ. He quickly agreed and said he wanted the same.

"How? How could you truly forgive me?" He said he had just like Christ had. That statement took my breath away. Only God.

We lived in different states, so he came to visit me, I visited him, we talked on the phone, and texted a lot. I was going to be baptized and wanted him to witness that special day. He said he wouldn't miss it and brought our son with him. We all had a wonderful weekend of restoration and time together. The time went by too fast and we both longed for more.

I knew it was important for Robert and the kids to watch me over a long period of time to see the change in me. I needed them to watch how I responded to life, and how I lived my life since I became a Christian. I needed them to be able to trust me over time. I wanted everyone that I had deceived to watch my life, to see the transformation only found in Christ. I was convicted to call old friends and send a few emails to people I know I had hurt when I divorced. I needed to seek forgiveness for my sin. I sought forgiveness from family members from both sides I had hurt so terribly.

I truly was a different person. God saved me. He changed me from the inside out. As Romans 6:6–7 says, "We know that our old self was crucified with him in order that the body of sin might be brought to nothing, so that we would no longer be enslaved to sin. For the one who has died has been set free from sin."

Several months into our reconnecting, Robert asked a friend if he knew of someone that would mentor me as a new creation in Christ. Thankfully, God brought an incredible friend and mentor to me. Tamra was a gal who had previous experience in some of the same areas of sin I had been involved with. She was wise and kind. We spent every single Saturday morning on the phone for a year. She gave me books to read, scripture to memorize, she kept me accountable for my time with Jesus, she encouraged me and "spanked me" when I needed it. She helped keep my eyes on Jesus, not on Robert. She helped make sure my motives were sincere with him. She, as well as our children, didn't want him to get hurt again. "Over a long period of time" I kept telling myself. This is about God this time, not me. Maybe God didn't even want us to reconcile. Maybe it was just to forgive one another and move on. Only He knew.

Months later, at Robert's suggestion, I moved to California. Was it really God's will for us to remarry? You know when God is in control of a situation. There was no doubt it was God's will for me to move back. He provided a good job and an awesome place to live. His provision was perfect. I had the pleasure of moving in with my mom's cousin Dee. She lived five miles from Robert. Wow, God doesn't make mistakes! The time I had with Dee was such an encouragement. She was loving, encouraging, kind, and loved Jesus. She took a huge interest in my life and offered me great wisdom and advice. I know God allowed that time for me to grow in my faith and used Dee to lovingly mentor me.

After almost a year of "dating," we knew we were to remarry. We both knew that God had brought us together again to reconcile and restore our marriage and family. I still can't even think about that without tearing up and getting goosebumps! The time we had living in the same area again proved our love and commitment to Christ and each other—and was a true blessing. We got reacquainted with one another, went to church together, had incredible spiritual conversations, spent time with our children, walked the beach, and talked about God's grace and forgiveness. We intentionally set out to be the best example of Christ's love and redemption as we lived our lives for Him! On January 23, 2015, at the El Segundo, California, courthouse—with our children at our side—we remarried.

The divorce wasn't easy on either of our children, but when I came back to California it was especially difficult for our son Dylan. He was really mad when I came back and was super angry and disrespectful, and I deserved it. The example I was before Jesus saved me gave him no reason to ever trust me, no reason to trust my conversion was real, I was responsible for breaking up our family.

During the first few months of me being around Robert and Dylan (our daughter still lived in Arizona), Robert was amazingly kind and helpful. It was very important to him that Dylan see the change and encouraged me to not give up trying to restore our once very-strong relationship. When the three of us were out together, Robert would intentionally hang back and walk slowly so Dylan and I would be forced to walk together and talk. As God would allow, over a long period of time, Dylan began to see that I truly wasn't the same and finally let me in. He often says how great it is to have his "Mama" back. Oh, what a joy! We have a fantastic relationship today. As we modeled Christ in our marriage, our children have seen what restoration and redemption look like.

Our daughter was loving and supportive of our remarriage from the start. She knew I never stopped loving her dad and she wanted her family reconciled too. The divorce was hard on our children in different ways. I think it may have had the most lasting effect on Celeste. I was a terrible example of unconditional love, commitment, and marriage, and I'm pretty sure I didn't give her much hope for her own future. When she and I lived together after the divorce, I became her friend more than her mother. I was so lost and just wanted us to get along and be happy. And yet, I knew I had the responsibility to guide her, but what I was doing was actually failing her. She was only 15 when we moved to Arizona. New state, new school, new friends, no dad, and no brother. She and I had few very tumultuous yet loving years. In the final stages of the Lord getting ahold of my heart, she was there. She was with me when God brought me to my knees. How she loved me through that will never be forgotten.

I have terrible regret and sadness when I think of how our children suffered for my sin and yet I know God will use it for His glory and our good. I also cling to Romans 8:1, "There is therefore now no condemnation for those who are in Christ Jesus," and our children are able to see Christ in me. We have our children's trust and respect and they know that in all things we will follow Jesus and not our sinful flesh. We continue to pray for our children and grandchildren to put their faith and trust in Jesus, as we live our lives for Him daily. I tell them that no matter what they can't out sin God. No matter the sin, no matter the time, when you repent of your sins and follow Christ, He will take you in His loving arms for eternity.

The fullness of our marriage today isn't at all how it was before. It's not about stuff, status, or anything other than Christ. It's about dying to self—to show and demonstrate selfless love. God's love for us and our love for each other is rich and full. It's honest and joyful. My husband leads me well and I fully submit to his leadership, which wasn't the old Zoe. The unsaved Zoe was selfish, prideful, and super-controlling. One of the books that my mentor had me read before we even considered remarriage, was Fierce Women by Kimberly Wagner. What an eye-opener; read it. The old Zoe was truly fierce.

Even in my sin and through all the terrible mistakes, one of the most amazing ways my husband has shown love and grace to me is by never saying a word about the time we were apart. He never blamed me, held anything against me, said unkind words about the choices and decisions I made, or how they impacted our family. Not once! And trust me, there was plenty of ammunition. He truly is a man of God. I often call him my Superman.

We are growing in God's grace together daily. We love and trust one another. We spend time in God's Word together and I marvel at how well he leads me and how much I love surrender and submission.

The fullness of our love is 100 percent God. All things are possible for those that love God, as long as it aligns with His perfect will. I thank God daily for the life he gave—the hard times, the sinful decisions, all of it—because it brought me to my knees in full repentance, and I daily need my Savior. The Lord has given me joy beyond belief and a contentment I've never known. I am completely content in Christ.

Robert and Zoe and children, Celeste and Dylan

Robert and Zoe Jones
2019

HOPE & HELPS

<u>Zoe</u>

Scripture I clung to on the hardest days/nights:

- Job 42:2. You can't thwart God's plan. No matter what, under whatever circumstances, we can't thwart His plan for our lives. When I got saved, I clung to this, knowing He was and is in total control of my life. It's a verse I use when counseling. It's a great hope for all who want someone they love to be saved.

- James 1:5–6. I didn't want to make any more mistakes, I didn't and still don't trust myself, so I constantly pray for wisdom and discernment. I know God gives that freely when we seek His will. I used to text my mentor, Tamra, to ask what I should do, how I should handle something. Her response, which at the time really frustrated me, was, "Go to the Throne, before the phone." Ugh. I really hated that! It was right and so wise of her! I went to my Bible, prayed, and asked for wisdom. Seek God's will—His wisdom, not another person!

Helpful things people did to minister to me:

- Prayed and prayed and prayed!

- Counseled and encouraged me.

- Held me accountable in a gentle manner.

- Gave me scripture and books to read to strengthen my faith.

- Sought me out at church to give me a big hug.

What you should NOT say to someone in a similar circumstance:

- Don't encourage people in their sin! I had several people encourage me in my sinful decisions.

- Don't sympathize with sinners. Their story probably isn't accurate.

Hymns or songs that comforted me:

- *Amazing Grace,* John Newton

- Instead of music, I listened to podcasts of incredible preachers, teachers, and encouragers. I couldn't get enough of God's Word. I sought expository preachers and clung to every word. My weekly/daily favorites are:

  o John MacArthur, Grace to You

  o Adam Bailie, Christ Church, Gilbert, Arizona

  o Journeywomen podcast

  o Daily Grace podcast

The hope Jesus has given me through my trial:
Hope in Jesus is everything. Without it there is nothing to live for, nothing to put your faith and trust in, nothing to long for. Without Jesus there will be an emptiness that will never get filled. Your cup will never be full.

The other hope we found through this incredible trial is that it is never too late to find Him. I was 50 years old. Never stop praying for an unsaved family member or friend. God is on the throne of grace and He longs for people to be saved. Never give up. We hope and pray that our children will too, one day, surrender their lives to Christ. The hope we have in Jesus is that we know, if they are chosen, they will one day live eternally with Him. Oh, what a joy that will be.

Robert

Scripture I clung to on the hardest days/nights:
1 Peter 5:10

Helpful things people did to minister to us:
- Prayed with me and for me.

- My parents' support had the greatest impact. They kept pointing me to the cross, no matter how I was feeling. They kept telling me to trust in the Lord. Trust in Him regardless of the circumstances.

- A few friends/family tried to confront the sin of my spouse (Matthew 18:15–20). Even when it doesn't restore the sinner, you have a biblical responsibility to confront sin. Few people feared God more than man in this regard.

What you should NOT say to someone in a similar circumstance:
- "This is just a season." Seasons can be long.

- Don't tell someone you are going to do something and then not do it. Be a man or woman of your word.

- "I know how you feel." Only say it if you truly know what someone is going through.

Hymns or songs that comforted me:
- *How Great Thou Art,* Carl Boberg. This carried me through years of sadness and loss.

- *Trust and Obey,* John Hammis. I never forgot this song from my youth and clung to it during this time.

The hope Jesus has given me through my trial:
Answered prayer continues to give me daily hope in so many ways: hope in the salvation of our children and grandchildren, hope in restored marriages all over the world. By God's amazing grace, nothing is impossible to those that love Christ.

Amazing Grace

A - maz - ing grace, how sweet the sound that
Twas grace that taught my heart to fear, and
Through ma - ny dan - gers, toils and snares, I
When we've been there ten thou - sand years, bright

saved a wretch like me. I once was
grace my fears re - lieved; How pre - cious
have al - rea - dy come; Tis grace hath
shin - ing as the sun. We've no less

lost but now am found; was blind but now I see.
did that grace a - ppear the hour I first be - lieved.
brought me safe thus far and grace will lead me home.
days to sing God's praise than when we first be - gun.

John Newton

So resist him, firm in your faith,
knowing that the same experiences of suffering
are being accomplished by your brothers and sisters
who are in the world.
After you have suffered for a little while,
the God of all grace,
who called you to His eternal glory in Christ,
will Himself perfect, confirm, strengthen,
and establish you.
To Him be dominion forever and ever.
Amen.

1 Peter 5:9–11

Who Is Like God

Emily Curtis

Who has known the mind of God,
Or numbered his own days?
Who can question any of His judgments,
Or give counsel to His ways?

He formed the beasts of earth,
And feeds them from His hand,
He told the waters of their boundaries,
And has numbered grains of sand.

His mighty voice was all it took to make the moon and stars,
So how can we, merely dust, think control is ours?

Is not He the source of wisdom and the giver of all things?
He has intricately painted sunsets and given flight to wings.
He formed each man while he was yet hidden in the womb.
He alone can give the breath of life,
And raise the dead up from the tomb.

Who are we to offer anything but praise,
And humbly bow before Him, submitting to His ways?

Oh, the depth of the riches, both of the wisdom and knowledge of God!
How unsearchable are His judgments and unfathomable His ways!
[34]For who has known the mind of the Lord, or who became His counselor?
[35]Or who has first given to Him, that it would be paid back to him?
[36]For from Him, and through Him, and to Him are all things.
To Him be the glory forever. Amen.

Romans 11:33–36

LIGHT IN THE DARKNESS
A SURE AND STEADY GOSPEL HOPE

But sanctify Christ as Lord in your hearts, always being ready
to make a defense to everyone who asks you to give an account
for the hope that is in you, yet with gentleness and reverence.

———

1 Peter 3:15

Our world is weighed down with sin and its many devastating consequences: fear, worry, pain, tears, guilt, and death. Our hearts long to be free from the troubles of this world and to experience the peace with God that humanity once knew. Although we do still see many great things in this world—beauty still exists, and peace can still be enjoyed to a degree—we are left yearning for something more day after day.

Good news seems to be outweighed by bad news. Harmony seems to be silenced by division. The joy of life is often drowned out by the guarantee of death. But if we look closer at Romans 6:23, we see that sin and death do not have the final say: "The wages of sin is death, but the free gift of God is eternal life in Christ Jesus our Lord." We have a hope, and His name is Jesus. Even though death entered the world because of Adam's sin, we can find everlasting comfort because of the work that was accomplished by Jesus Christ (Romans 5:17). God came and paid the price to rescue us from our sin. He came to earth in the person of His Son, Jesus (John 1:14). He did what we could never do by living a life of perfect obedience to God the Father (Philippians 2:8; Romans 5:19). And although He was crucified on a cross for our sins and was buried, He rose from the grave and ascended to heaven (1 Corinthians 15:3–4; Acts 1:9–11).

Later on in Romans, the apostle Paul reminds us of this great truth: God has done what we could never do (Romans 8:2–4). Through His unfolding plan and purposes, He made a way for us to have new life, eternal life. John 3:16–17 says, "God so loved the world, that he gave his only Son, that whoever believes in him should not perish but have eternal life. For God did not send his Son into the world to condemn the world, but in order that the world might be saved through him." When we read these truths in the Bible, we can't stop at intellectual assent. It's one thing to comprehend the

meaning of words and phrases. But the belief we read of in John 3:16—indeed, that we read of all throughout the Bible—involves a choice. Saving faith requires trusting God and committing one's life to Him alone. Has that struck you? Are you ready to make that choice? If so, there are a few simple steps you can take in response. We first have to acknowledge that there's something to admit—that you and I have sinned against God and could never make up for our wrongdoing. Second, we must believe that Jesus has taken on the penalty for our sins and conquered death once and for all. Finally, we must consider the implications of placing our faith in God. Admitting and believing has to be followed by obedience and repentance. The rest of our days will be spent turning away from sin and towards God, by the help of His Spirit (John 14:15–17). This is a transformation that touches every facet of life.

The good that was once known is gone. The bad now lingers and toils in vain. The new has come, offering us redemption. Yet still we await something better than we can fathom. … Imagine a world with no more tears, death, pain, or mourning. That's exactly what we read about in Revelation 21. God has promised to restore the broken world in which we live. It will be nothing less than perfection. Adam and Eve once experienced the goodness of life in God's presence. So too will all who place their faith in the Lord Jesus, for the dwelling place of God once again will be with man (Revelation 21:1–4). For now, though, we wait patiently, eagerly anticipating eternal life with Christ as we joyfully obey all that He has commanded in His Word.

Alistair Begg
Senior Pastor, Parkside Church

RESOURCES
TO ENCOURAGE THOSE
WHO ARE MOURNING

BOOKS

- *Safe in the Arms of God*, John MacArthur
- *What Grieving People Wish You Knew about What Really Helps (and What Really Hurts)*, Nancie Guthrie (for family and friends of the grieving to read)
- *Gentle and Lowly*, Dane Ortlund
- *And Still She Laughs*, Kate Merrick
- *A Symphony in the Dark*, Barbara Rainey and Rebecca Rainey Mutz
- *Spurgeon's Sorrows*, Zane Eswine
- *Hope When It Hurts*, Kristen Wetherell and Sarah Walton
- *Trusting God*, Jerry Bridges
- *The Moon Is Always Round*, Jonathan Gibson and Joe Hox
- *All Things for Good*, Thomas Watson
- *Beside Bethesda: 31 Days Toward Deeper Healing*, Joni Eareckson Tada
- *Suffering and the Sovereignty of God*, John Piper
- *Suffering*, Paul David Tripp
- *Dark Valleys*, Todd Smith (for those suffering depression)
- *Grace Like Scarlett*, Adriel Booker (for miscarriage and loss)
- *A Grace Disguised*, Jerry Sittser
- *Marriage, Remarriage and Divorce*, Jay Adams
- *Just Show Up*, Kara Tippetts and Jill Lynn Buteyn (for family and friends to read)
- *When God Doesn't Make Sense*, James Dobson
- *The Path of Loneliness*, Elizabeth Elliot
- *Unmet Expectations*, Lisa Hughes
- *Songs of Suffering*, Joni Eareckson Tada

HYMNS

The hymns in this book can be listened to on our website hopeinthemourning.com.

TANGIBLE GIFTS & GESTURES

- Custom gifts that include their loved one's name, birthstone or picture
- Christmas ornament that they can use each year to remember their loved one
- Bringing meals. Consider adding in a few groceries for breakfasts as well
- Blankets, coffee, tea, warm slippers. Things that bring warmth and comfort
- Keepsake boxes
- Cards sent on meaningful days (birthday, anniversary, Christmas, day of death)
- Housecleaning services in the local area
- Offer to babysit children. Consider giving a gift card for a dinner out as well
- Scripture, quotes or poems written on 3x5 cards
- Writing journal to record memories or write letters to their loved one
- Offer to help with funeral arrangements, phone calls and scheduling
- A listening ear and shoulder to cry on are so valuable. Don't hesitate to hug and cry with them
- Check in frequently with those who have long term illness and offer meals or child care
- Lawn care
- Offer to wash and fold laundry. It's best to say "I'd like to come help with laundry, what day can I come this week?" This makes them feel less like a burden and makes your offer more genuine and likely to be utilized
- Come to their home and water flower arrangements (especially after a funeral)
- Be available and willing to change your schedule to accommodate their needs
- Say their loved one's name and share memories of them as they come to mind. It's nice to know that they are remembered and loved; the grieving person is thinking of them often so don't be afraid to mention them.

- Bring homemade cookies or bread
- If applicable, offer to bring kids to and from school
- Financial gifts can help offset high medical expenses and lessen a large burden
- Phone calls and visits. Keep visits short. 15-20 minutes is best. Remember that they are likely exhausted and a short visit is most loving.
- Pray with and for them often. If you say "I'll be praying for you", stop and pray right then so you don't forget.
- Make a point to engage with them when you see them. Don't avoid interactions. Listen attentively. Remember that there is more too them than their trial.
- Invite them to activities. Even if they don't come, keep inviting them. Have grace and patience
- Music CDs with rich, meaningful music and lyrics, such as:
  - *The Glorious Unfolding*, Steven Curtis Chapman
  - *Beauty Will Rise*, Steven Curtis Chapman
  - *Scripture Lullabies*, volumes 1, 2, and 3
  - *Bring Your Nothing*, Shane and Shane
  - *Blessings*, Laura Story
  - *The Burning Edge of Dawn*, Andrew Peterson
  - *Resurrection Letters*, Andrew Peterson
  - *Evensong*, Keith and Kristyn Getty
  - *Quintology—Passion*, Keith and Kristyn Getty
- Gift cards for:
  - gas
  - groceries
  - coffee
  - restaurants
  - massage
  - Amazon
  - family portraits with a local photographer

Climbing the Mountain

Excerpts from a Charles Spurgeon Sermon

Behold, then, before your eyes believer, the hill of God; This mount of which we speak is not Mount Sinai, but the chosen hill whereon are gathered the glorious company of angels, the spirit of the just made perfect, the Church of the first-born, whose names are written in heaven. And we are the pilgrims making our way to the top of God's mountain, full often joyous with faith, but sometimes weary and footsore.

You may say, "I shall never ascend the hill of God for I am weak, and the hill is exceeding high; too lofty to be attained by tottering feet like mine. I am so sore tried, the road is very rough … my bones ache, my knees bend, my head is giddy, and I drag my bleeding feet with anguish from crag to crag."

Oh! my dear brother, be of good cheer; if that be thine only cause of mourning, lay it aside, for remember, whilst thou art weak, it is not thy strength which is to carry thee there, but God's. If nature had undertaken to ascend into the celestial mountain, indeed, you might despair; but it is grace, all-conquering grace that is to do it.

It is true the hill is steep, but then God is omnipotent, it is certain that the Alp is high, but higher still is the love and grace of God. He hath borne you, he hath carried you, and he will carry you even to the end: when you cannot walk he will take you in his arms, and when the road is so rough that you cannot even creep along it, he will bear you as on eagles' wings, till he bring you to his promised rest.

Those stones and flints give foothold. Stand then, strong in the strength of God, and be of good courage. When you have nothing else to trust to, put your hand within the hand of the Eternal God, and he will wisely lead, and powerfully sustain you.

Look up, man; look up! The Scripture does not say, "Let us run with trembling the race that is set before us, looking to our own tottering legs;" no; but it says, "Let us run with patience the race that is set before us, looking unto Jesus." What if the crag be steep, and the precipice be grim; what is that to thee? You will never fall while your faith is fixed on your God! Look up to the Father of lights, with whom there is no variableness; he bids you silently look unto him, and stand securely.

Courage, pilgrim courage! Up that crag, man! Now put hand and knee to it—up!—for when you have climbed a little higher, ay, but a very little, you shall lie down to rest, and then no more fatigue or sorrow [or pain].

And, brethren, when we shall mount to the hill of God, what sights we shall see!

We shall see the King in his beauty. We shall behold his face; we shall look into his eyes, we shall drink love from the fountain of his heart.